37392

How to Get Up When Life Gets You Down

Books available from HarperCollins as Fount Paperbacks

by the same authors
THE GUIDE TO THE HERE AND HEREAFTER

by Lionel Blue
A BACKDOOR TO HEAVEN

How to Get Up When Life Gets You Down

A Companion and Guide

Lionel Blue and Jonathan Magonet

Fount

An Imprint of HarperCollins*Publishers*

To Daphne, Gordian, Mary and Wendy
LB

To Doro, Gavriel and Abigail
JM

231.8

HarperCollins*Religious*
Part of HarperCollins*Publishers*
77–85 Fulham Palace Road, London W6 8JB

First published in Great Britain
in 1992 by HarperCollins*Religious*

1 3 5 7 9 10 8 6 4 2

A catalogue record for this book
is available from the British Library

ISBN 0 00 215192 8 — 20022927

Printed and bound in Great Britain by
Hartnolls Limited, Bodmin, Cornwall

Acknowledgements

The author and publisher acknowledge with thanks permission to reproduce copyright material as listed below:

Associated University Presses, New Jersey, for the extract, "Adventure" from *The Burning Bush: Poems and Other Writings 1940–1980* (1983) by Aaron Kramer.

Atheneum Publishers, an imprint of Macmillan Publishing Company, for the poem "Nothing" from *The Static Element: Selected Poems of Natan Zach* (1982), translated by Peter Everwine and Shulamit Yasny-Starkman.

Blackwell Publishers, Oxford, and Cornell University Press, New York, for the extract from *Modernity and the Holocaust* (1989) by Zygmunt Bauman.

Bloch Publishing Company, New York, for the quotation from *Light and Salvation* by L I Rabinowitz (1965).

Carcanet Press Limited for the extract, "He and I" from *The Little Virtues* by Natalia Ginzburg (1982).

Columbia Picture Publications/Belwyn, 15800 NW 48th Ave, Miami, FL 33014, USA, for "Spring is Here First" by Ira Gershwin. Reproduced in the USA and Canada by permission.

Commentary magazine for "I cannot recall . . ." by Saul Gottlieb (1955).

EMI United Partnership Ltd for "Spring is Here First" by Ira Gershwin. Reproduced by Permission.

The Estate of Delmore Schwarz for "The Would-Be Hungarian" by Delmore Schwartz.

Hai & Topsy Frankl for the lyrics "My Little Son" by Morris Rosenfeld and "Schpil-she mir a Lidele in Jiddisch" by I. Kotliar, both published in *Jiddische Lieder* (1981, Fischer Taschenbuch Verlag).

HarperCollins for "Prophecy" by Allen Ginsberg from *White Shroud: Poems 1980–85* (1986, Perennial Library).

Hodder and Stoughton Limited, and Beacon Press Ltd in the USA, for the extract from *Man's Search for Meaning* (1955) by Viktor Frankl.

Hodder and Stoughton Limited and Putnam Publishing Group for the extract from *Gracie: A Love Story* (1989) by George Burns.

The Holocaust Library for the extract from *Ghetto Diary* (1978) by Janusz Korczak.

Jewish Chronicle for the poem "Deathbed in May" by Pamela Melnikoff.

Journal of Reform Judaism for "Singles gather together" by Norman Lipson (Summer 1988).

Dorothea Magonet for "The Experience of Conversion to Judaism" (*European Judaism*, Vol. 22, no. 1, issue 42).

Penguin Books Ltd for the extract from *Mr Sammler's Planet* (1971) by Saul Bellow.

Random Century Group and Uitgeverij Balans for the extract from *The Diary of Etty Hillesum*.

Warner Chappell Music Ltd for "Little Girl Blue", "I Wish I Were in Love Again", "Someone to Watch over Me" and "By Myself" by Lorenz Hart. Reproduced by permission.

Warner Chappell Music Inc, 9000 Sunset Boulevard, Penthouse, Los Angeles, CA 90069, USA, for permission to quote the above lyrics by Lorenz Hart in the USA and Canada.

How to Get Up When Life Gets You Down

George Weidenfeld & Nicolson Ltd and African International Productions for the extract from *Prisoner Without A Name, Cell Without A Number* (1981) by Jacobo Timmerman.

George Weidenfeld & Nicolson Ltd for the extract from *Fear No Evil – A Memoir* (1988) by Natan Sharansky.

Harriet Wistrich for "Amongst all the anguish and troubles . . ." by Ewa Wistrich.

Every effort has been made to trace copyright owners, and the publishers apologize to anyone whose rights have inadvertently not been acknowledged. This will be corrected in any reprint.

Other Sources

Judaism by Arthur Hertzberg (1962, Washington Square Press, an imprint of Simon & Schuster).

"Art and Meaning" by Yehuda Bacon (World Union for Progressive Judaism Youth Section. Pamplet no. 3)

The words of Rav Abraham Isaac Kook are quoted by Herbert Weiner in the Proceedings of the Central Conference of American Rabbis, 1964.

Reflections in a Pumpkin Field by Jay R Brickman (1989, Montgomery Media Inc).

"Letter to Sophie Liebknecht" by Rosa Luxemburg is quoted in *My Country is the Whole World: An Anthology of Women's Work on Peace and War* by the Cambridge Women's Peace Collective (Pandora Press). First translated in *Letters from Prison* (1923 Eden & Cedar Paul). Republished in Independent Labour Party/Square One Pamphlets (1972, London).

"To Be an Arab Jew" by Nava Mizrahhi is quoted in *The Tribe of Dina: A Jewish Women's Anthology*, edited by Melanie Kay-Kantrowitz and Irena Klepfisz (1986, *Sinister Wisdom* 29/30).

Yes I Can: The Story of Sammy Davis Jr by Sammy Davis Jr and Jane and Burt Boyar (1966, Farrar, Straus & Giroux Inc.).

"The Rosenberg Case: We Are All Your Children" by Vicki Gabriner, was published in *Chutzpah: A Jewish Liberation Anthology* (1977, New Glide Publications).

"Reflections on the Myth of Marriage" by Abraham Barzeli was published in *Harvest*, a magazine of the Analytical Psychology Club of London (28, 1982).

Change Lobsters and Dance by Lilli Palmer (1977, A Star Book, Macmillan Publishers Ltd).

"A Future Without a Perhaps" by Gabriel Preil from *Sunset Possibilities and Other Poems* translated and with an introduction by Robert Friend (1985, Jewish Publication Society of America).

"Like A Mousetrap" and "You Shouldn't Be Taken Aback" from *Selected Poems of Yankev Glatshteyn*, edited by Richard J Fein (1987, Jewish Publication Society of America).

Shalom Aleichem is quoted in *Voices of Wisdom – Jewish Ideals and Ethics for Everyday Living* by Frances Klagsburn (1980, Pantheon Books, a division of Random House Inc.).

Bob Dylan: Writings and Drawings (1974, Grandada Publishing Ltd).

Contents

Contents

Preface

When we were looking for a possible topic for a book to follow up our *Guide to the Here and Hereafter*, Lionel immediately thought of the subject of suffering. It is a central issue of human life, and the one which most challenges any simple or comfortable belief in a benign God. It seemed also, at first glance, to lend itself to the sort of format of the previous book – a selection of powerful quotations from Jewish sources, "ancient and modern", tied loosely together with a brief linking commentary.

But pretty soon it became clear that the links and explanations about our choice of passages became more and more important – and that the scope and range of the book was potentially enormous. We also began to recognize the limitations on what we could legitimately offer to others out of our own experience. We have both knocked about the world a bit and suffered the average wear and tear on our bodies, our relationships and our souls that most twentieth-century people experience. We have both had a good religious training, formally at the same Rabbinic seminary, informally in the ongoing power of our own relationship with God and the friends and colleagues, of many religions and none, who have been our teachers. We have also experienced personal crises of different sorts that have had effects on our own way of viewing the world and our life. But there are overwhelming catastrophes that occur to people – natural disasters, wars, disabling or destroying illnesses, persecution or forced emigration – that are far beyond our personal experience. For being spared such things we can say a heartfelt "Thank you" to God, but it does lessen our credentials in compiling a book that recognizes that suffering is the inevitable lot of all human beings, but tries to ask how we can learn to live with it, cope with it, and grow through and beyond it.

In some ways, the use of the anthology material is a helpful device. We may not have been there personally, but many people have, and have brought back a record of their experience to offer to others. Survivors of concentration camps, those who have had to face the death of a child, others coming to terms with their own imminent death – many have tried to offer some comfort to others out of their experience – and somehow, in the process itself, transform their own horror, fear or bitterness into something that can become life-affirming and of value. If we have strayed beyond our own personal experience, it is because they have been in some measure our teachers and we have been able to pass on what they have taught us.

If we have any expertise, it is in the common human reality that we are each of us in many ways our own worst enemy. We do not need to go far beyond our own envy, jealousies, pettiness and self-destructive anger, our feelings of inadequacy and failure, to reach the heart of so much of human suffering. The search for love and coping with personal loss are the sources of our suffering as much as the catastrophes and disasters that fall upon us from without. Perhaps the greatest thing that a book like this can achieve is to enable readers to discover and acknowledge their own expertise in coping with life and write their own personal chapter on the lessons they have learnt and the guidance they can give to others.

What is the religious dimension to all of this? We have used materials from biblical sources or Jewish tradition, though far less than in our previous book. I am not altogether sure why. Though they offer an inexhaustible mine of materials, they do not always speak as directly as the anecdotes and poems and experiences of people living this century and sharing our common uncertainties about the meaning of life and the reality of God. In some situations the self-confident pronouncements of our tradition are comforting and reassuring – in others their very certainty disturbs and confuses. There is an entire theological discipline, "theodicy", which attempts to understand the role of God in a world of suffering, but formal academic studies offer little comfort when suffering afflicts us.

Much of what Lionel writes here is aimed at exploring the presence of God in our lives at such critical junctures – and how we build the habits of addressing and seeking God in all circumstances, of making our behaviour "Godly". If that experience is part of us there is no guarantee we will not experience suffering, but we have access to God's strength and consolation when we meet it. The Hebrew Bible, in a most unexpected way, reminds us that we have to "train" ourselves to "fear" God. We are not to be like slaves who live in guilt and dread of a cruel master, but perhaps we are to be like apprentices who learn from serving and living in the presence of our teacher. But we are also commanded to "love" God, with all our heart, soul and might. So that all that we know of "love" – falling in love, making love, seeking love, earning love; its joys and fears, disappointments and self-sacrifice, yearning and jealousy, follies and absurdities – all these are clues to that other love that can take us to unexpected heights and depths on a journey without end.

There is a story I learned when studying in Heidelberg. It seems that a Professor of Ethics lived a singularly unethical life. When challenged on the gap between what he taught and how he lived, he replied: "Have you ever seen a signpost walking in the direction in which it is pointing?" In this book we cannot afford to be so split. We have tried to give from our experience and only reach beyond it where we can rely on the experience of others to guide us. If the title seems a bit flippant, especially for those in the throes of real personal suffering, we apologize in advance. But suffering is there to be met by us all, and part of our problem today is that too much of our culture is designed to hide that reality from us so that we meet it totally unprepared, and the very denial of its existence does us even more damage. If religion has a task in a secular world, it is to encourage us to accept such reality, and then try to move beyond it. In secular terms we can seek its meaning for us so that it can be transformed into something positive. In religious terms, it may be that as well, but somehow also a key to the mystery of our life and the unique task that has been assigned us by our Creator.

Jonathan Magonet

P.S.
We have tried to explain special Jewish terms as we have used them. The only exception is the word Hasid (plural Hasidim) which refers to a Jewish spiritual movement which began in the eighteenth century in Eastern Europe.

In speaking of God we have retained the conventional "He". It could equally be "She".

I

Little Things That Get You Down

I

"People are born to trouble . . ."

(JOB 5:7)

A hunter once caught a bird. It told him: "Set me free and I'll teach you three wise rules: Never regret that which is past, never believe the unbelievable, never reach for the unattainable."

The hunter let the bird go free and it flew to the top of a tree. Then it thanked him and told him: "I have a pearl within me worth a million gold pieces!"

Regretting his generosity the hunter climbed up the tree to catch the bird, fell and broke his neck.

The bird mocked him: "You have not learned anything from my teaching. I am free now – why regret the past? I am so small, how could I have such a huge pearl within me? I warned you not to reach for the unattainable, yet you tried to reach the top of this tree!"

That story comes from a medieval Jewish collection of wise stories and it shows the problem of trying to hand on the wisdom of the past. The great Jewish teachers had a lot to say about suffering – most of it wise, helpful and appropriate. The snag is that much of what they say only makes sense or helps us if we already come to the same conclusion – usually through the painful route of our own mistakes and experience.

The Book of Job in the Bible is the story of an honest man who suffered terribly and struggled to understand what was happening to him – he wasn't helped by his friends who tried to sell him a lot of secondhand wisdom. So one of his earliest conclusions was that suffering is simply part of being human: "People are born to trouble as surely as sparks fly upward" (*Job 5:7*).

Many centuries later a rabbi turned it round: "Not to

know suffering means not to be a human being" (*Genesis Rabbah 92:1*).

In the Middle Ages, the great poet and philosopher Solomon Ibn Gabirol pushed the point a stage further:

> To believe that no misfortune will befall you, is like wishing not to live at all, for misfortunes are a necessary part of this transient world.

The rabbis tried to figure out at least some basic reasons for human suffering. The most obvious was the idea of Job's friends – a sort of cause and effect view of the way of the world. If you suffer, you must have done something wrong – though Job did not think much of that argument. Nevertheless the rabbis suggested that the first thing we should do is look at our past behaviour.

Rava said:

> If someone experiences much suffering, he or she should examine their deeds. If this shows they have sinned in some way, they should repent. If this examination reveals nothing, then they should attribute their sufferings to their neglect of study of the Torah, God's teaching. If this is still not the case, then they should know that their sufferings are "afflictions of love", as it is written, "Everyone in whom God delights, He crushes with sufferings"
> (*Isaiah 53:10*).

They explained this further with the image of two pots, one cracked, one whole – you don't tap the cracked one as you know it will break, but the sound one you will tap, presumably to show its soundness (*Genesis Rabbah 32:3*). Again this may not be particularly comforting, but it begins to bring God into the picture and suggests that though there may not be any acceptable reason for suffering, some meaning may eventually be found within it.

That, at least, is the witness of some – but not all – of the survivors of the concentration camps. The Israeli artist

"People are born to trouble . . ." (Job 5:7)

Yehudah Bacon survived the camps as a child. For years afterwards he used to paint stark black and white illustrations of his experience until he realized that people did not really want to know. Later he came under the influence of Martin Buber and was able to explain things this way:

> It was much later that I really understood the meaning of suffering. It can have a meaning if it changes you for the better. As I learnt from Martin Buber, the Hasidim say there are two forms of suffering: one has a positive influence and the other a negative. How do you tell the difference? Suffering from God teaches you something, and suffering from evil drags you down. Of course, at the time of suffering you don't see this.
>
> One of the greatest things it can teach us is a greater understanding of other human beings. It is so basic that it shakes you to your soul and therefore it shows you yourself and the reality of "self" in other people – it opens your eyes to the reality of other human beings which you would never otherwise understand. Because of this you can come to understand even your oppressors somehow. I don't say we have to learn understanding in this way, but it is one of the positive results of suffering.
>
> Yehudah Bacon in "Art and Meaning"

Two Hasidic masters, both of whom suffered greatly in their lives from their own internal torments, have left teachings about the inevitability of suffering and what one might try to do with it.

Nachman of Bratzlav taught:

> The truth is that the world is full of woes. There is no one who really possesses this world. Even the greatest magnates and princes do not truly possess this world, because their days are filled with upsets and pain, with disturbances and sadness, and every one has his own particular woe.
>
> *Judaism* Ed. Arthur Hertzberg

Mendel of Kotzk, the Kotzker Rebbe, was a very austere, even harsh, figure, deeply committed to the search for truth.

He spent the last twenty years of his life in seclusion and is far removed from the rather sentimental picture we tend to have of the great Hasidic leaders. The lesson the following story about him teaches, comes close to the ideas in Lionel's next section:

> A man once came to Rabbi Mendel of Kotzk to pour out his bitter heart. His wife had died in childbirth leaving him with seven young children including the newly-born infant. He had other woes too and did not know where to turn.
>
> Rabbi Mendel listened to him, but while listening the rabbi kept his eyes lowered. After a moment of deep meditation Rabbi Mendel raised his head, looked straight into the eyes of the petitioner and said: "I am not equal to the task of consoling you after such cruel suffering. Only the true Master of mercy is equal to that. Turn to him."   *Judaism* Ed. Arthur Hertzberg

JM

2

The art of giving up

Losses can easily fester inside us. Even small ones can poison our soul. Now I'm not good at machines and only learnt to drive late. I practised in a hotted-up mini, urged on by advanced motorist friends, who impressed upon me the importance of "flair".

Well, I certainly drove with a certain something, which impressed the Jags and Mercs my mini overtook.

When I stopped at traffic lights, making wild hand signals, one of them pulled alongside me, put out his hand, and shook mine. I still wonder what he meant.

I bet a colleague I'd pass the test before him. Well, I had five goes, he had six, but I wore my dog collar which he said wasn't fair. But I said it wasn't fair, when I backed into a garage painted green like the lawn. Then he said it wasn't his fault a collie dog crossed the road, during his hundred point turn.

It wasn't a collie but a cow which nearly scuppered me – a highway code cow. "What would you do, if you met a cow at night on a country lane?"

"Stop!" I said. Silence. "Well, what do you want me to do, milk it?" To my surprise, I passed – perhaps it was that dog collar.

But driving's out for the next few years, because I've had a blackout, and after all that effort, it feels like a bereavement. It leaves behind the same self-pity and anger, which I have to flush out of my system, before they do me more damage than the loss of any driving licence.

But how? I've no mystic cure-all, only some ways which have worked for me and friends.

If I think of cousins in concentration camps who would

have given their all to suffer my little loss, the feeling of unfairness goes. It's crude but effective.

I also remember a sermon I gave about Life. Life wasn't designed for happiness, I said, but for learning, and it taught two lessons. One was the art of giving, and the other the art of giving up. The second lesson was harder but not optional. It was compulsory, since we all die with nothing.

I also make God a present of my losses, which sounds daft, but works. At the end of the day I recite all my failures and disappointments. And then I mentally roll them up in a ball and call out to God. "Catch!" I say, and throw the black ball away from me to Him. He must do just that, for I never think of most of them again.

I also project my problems on to friends in the jokey Jewish way. Two friends meet after many years, and chat. Then one says sadly, "You haven't once asked me how's your business?"

"I'm sorry," said the other, "How is your business?"

"Don't ask!" he moaned.

But you may have to ask. Perhaps you suffered your little loss when the stock market wobbled. Perhaps your pension took a knock, or you're stuck with a mortgaged home you can't sell.

I've no cure-all as I've said, but these ways may help you clean up the inner mess your little loss has left in you. And if, by the way, you meet a highway code cow at night in a country lane, do ring the police!

LB

3

Finding God in tense times

In tense times, people not unnaturally turn to God, but that's easier said than done. "Where can I find God, for religious rituals have gone dead on me?" becomes a practical not an academic question.

It's happened to me too. I couldn't find Him either in all the old familiar places. Now the prophet Jeremiah said play holy hide-and-seek with Him. "'If you seek Me you will find Me. If you seek Me with your whole heart, I shall let you find Me' says the Lord."

Tracking Him down seemed to me more like a holy treasure hunt than hide-and-seek, and two incidents provided the clues.

The first took place in the waiting room at the end of a hospital ward. The doctors were doing their rounds, so I sat waiting with two women. One woman fumbled with her handbag, the other smoked cigarette after cigarette. They weren't aware of each other.

Then Sister poked her head in and beckoned to Cigarette. "You can see your husband now Mrs So-and-so – I'm afraid you'll find him rather sleepy." Cigarette went out and returned ten minutes later. She hesitated and then went over to Handbag, which intrigued me, and impulsively tapped her on the arm. "Your turn now. No, I won't come in with you. See him alone." Handbag, looking astonished, scuttled out, while Cigarette sat on motionless. Something significant had happened, but what?

Later on I learnt that the man was dying. Cigarette was his wife, Handbag his mistress.

I'd witnessed an act of spontaneous generosity. Cigarette had let God get into the act as well as her rival, and I don't think she would ever regret it. The glow certainly remained with me for months.

That incident made me think of a funeral on the Continent. The mourners were grave, the prayers moving, and the sermon solemn, theological rather than personal, in the continental manner. It was a cold day and the rawness of death made me shiver.

Later on I learnt the deceased had AIDS, though this was never mentioned. Not mentioned either were his friend and his buddy, both of whom had been discreetly advised to stay away, though it was they who had nursed him, wiped away the sweat from his face and held him tight when he felt hopeless.

God must have been with them, when they nursed him, I thought, otherwise they couldn't have done it. But like them, I don't think He attended that funeral either, which accounted for my sense of desolation.

A rabbinic story helped me interpret these two clues. A rabbi was asked, "Where does God live?", the same question, in another form, that I mentioned before. "Wherever a human being lets Him in," he answered.

And I would add two things I learnt from these incidents. His presence brings no quick worldly triumphs – just the glow I mentioned – and the password to His presence is generosity. So it's up to you whether you want to pay the price and let Him into your life – advice which is hard but hopeful.

LB

4

Bores

I remember a girl I met at a party in my early twenties. Apart from being tall and quite attractive she stood out from the crowd by wearing mid-thigh-length leather boots – like she'd just stepped off the stage of a panto. She told me she was an existentialist. I asked what that meant and she explained that her philosophy in life was not to be bored and not to bore other people. Alas, she hardly lived up to the latter intention. I last saw her at the end of the evening, squinting into a cracked mirror, trying to repair her mascara.

She bored me, I suppose, because her entire conversation was about herself, not me – I was just a convenient ear. If she hadn't been so attractive – and the boots helped a lot – I'd have escaped a lot sooner.

I suspect that this is not the most charitable of attitudes to take. But the way we feel about people who irritate or bore us is a very good test of our generosity of spirit. On the scales of human suffering, being stuck in a situation with someone who gets to you in that way, with no way out, hardly rates very high – but at times it can be a miserable enough experience. A fellow existentialist, Jean-Paul Sartre, locked three such characters up in a room together in a play for the whole of eternity. He concluded that "Hell is other people."

But if we are to see how we cope with suffering, perhaps it is best to start with something relatively easy like this and see how we deal with it. A good example that I find difficult to cope with is being stuck next to someone in a plane who insists on talking when all I want to do is sleep or finish my detective story. The following poem was written as a way of exorcising just such an occasion. It is not very kind, I'm afraid, but writing it at the time was a creative way of getting rid of my more violent feelings. A good bit of literary invective can work wonders.

To you, madam,
my neighbour on Pan Am Flight 101
Heathrow to JFK
Cabin class, I dedicate this poem.
And to your husband.
French?
A dentist – he will lecture soon in Paris
– who listened with such patience
to your opening forty-minute tirade.

Yes, you were definitely booked in seat 6F,
an aisle seat,
Clipper class,
arranged before you left New York.
Yes you did want to sit next to him
but could he not understand that you meant
on each side of the aisle
not scrunched up in a middle seat
especially among these yokels from the country
on some cheap package flight
when you had paid the full fare!

And you had hoped to rest on this flight
to arrive in New York refreshed
for two seats at the opera tonight
Don Carlos
and you'd missed it twice before.
The first forty minutes of seven hours.
Between the pauses
when he slept or you slept
(you'd seen the movie on the flight out)
we heard the saga of his relations in Vienna,
the girl who nearly married the brother

of a Chinese airline pilot who only wanted
a mother for his two children.
And how could he be planning a new trip to Europe
at that very moment before they'd even landed
without asking you about it first
without leaving you space for yourself
to sort out your medical problems
a blood test
– the doctor had insisted –
and some more intimate internal trouble
you did not wish to discuss
at this moment in time,
and your swimming lessons,
newly begun,
and your decision generally to relax more,
to enjoy New York,
to "initiate a change" in your life.

In between the strident whine
cuddling him and cooing
and crossing and uncrossing
and lifting onto the seat ahead
and recrossing again
your extraordinary, demented,
restless legs,
skirt hitched up to the thighs.
(Clearly not Jewish but Protestant
said a sympathetic New York friend later
– the exposure of the legs, he explained.)
Such energy, such need,
such magnificently, unremitting,
blatant, self-centredness.
Wise to have picked a European husband.
You gobbled your in-flight food
(forgive my noticing
but everything was somehow on display)
evidence of an older, deeper hunger?

If you read this
take my advice
and double-check the blood pressure
but meanwhile
have a nice day.

Of course that is only half the story. How often have I made someone else's life utterly miserable by being the wrong person in the wrong place at the wrong time? Has someone ever had to write a poem like that about me? Whenever I think about that a line by Eugene Heimler comes back to me in which he is describing part of his experience in Buchenwald concentration camp. And suddenly I find it possible to become much more patient and tolerant towards that awkward person that I never wanted to meet:

When someone was despicable, greedy and selfish, I remembered all the occasions when I, too, had been despicable, greedy and selfish. Buchenwald taught me to be tolerant of myself, and by that means tolerant of others.

JM

5

If you're not wired up right

I want to tell you about a hero who survived military wars, to fight another spiritual war, my friend Travers.

You may remember him, for he was the actor who brought tears to your eyes, as the little boy in the film *Goodbye Mr Chips*.

Travers also brought tears to my eyes of a different sort – because his stories of his former drunken days were hilarious.

About fifty years ago, when he was playing Napoleon, he and a crony, who was playing a courtier, went off on a bender, and arrived back worse for wear at the theatre. The courtier went on first, tripped up over his sword, and fell into the Empress Josephine's lap. She prodded him with her imperial crown, he leapt off and goggled at the audience, who jeered. A man stood up in the stalls and shouted, "You're drunk!"

The courtier seemed to be enjoying some private joke. "You think I'm drunk?" he giggled.

"Yes," shouted the audience.

"Well, you wait till you've seen Napoleon," he said triumphantly – and collapsed, as Travers staggered on stage.

So Travers did not remain an actor. Instead he saved other drunks from D.T's, drowning in their own vomit and the dreaded shakes. He never minced matters. When someone asked what I was doing at an alcoholic retreat, for my problems lie in a different direction, Travers said succinctly, "Lionel isn't wired up right, just like us."

I lose things, I break things, and the milk bottle in the fridge jumps out at me. I have to go back home time after time to make sure the stove is turned off.

But though blunt, Travers was never brutal. He saw through the tricks people who aren't wired up right resort to – but he never blamed them. His last story to me was about some poor chain-smoking monk who asked his abbot, "Father, may I have your permission to smoke when I contemplate?"

"Of course not!"

The desperate monk tried again. "Well then may I have your permission to contemplate when I smoke?"

When you see things spiritually, they're never what they seem. In God's eyes, was Travers' handicap a handicap or blessing, when, because of it, so many addicts were released from hell?

I hope this gives you courage, if you too aren't wired up right, like him and me and millions of others – if you spill things, lose letters, and can't bring library books back in time, if you hit the bottle or bottles jump out at you.

O.K., so you aren't wired up right, for this world! Perhaps God's wired you up better for the next. Your handicap could be your door to heaven.

LB

6

Shyness and disapproval

I admire the way politicians absorb so much disapproval. We ministers of religion are not so good at it – we like to be liked too much. My poor pooch Re'ach dreaded disapproval, and evolved three strategies to prevent it – dear doggie, poor doggie and devout doggie.

Any new unknown got the dear doggie treatment. She licked him and flattered him rotten, till he felt like St Francis.

If he proved resistant, she tried poor doggie, cowering in a doorway and looking piteous.

Devout doggie was reserved for religious softies. She stood up gravely during prayers, with that constipated look which so easily passes for contemplation.

Only my former lodger Carlo could resist her winning ways. He was an expressionist, who hated dogs and Re'ach especially. She tried every trick, even creeping into his bed. When Carlo awoke, he felt something soft on his cheek and screamed expressionistically. It was raw liver – Re'ach's love offering. He ate his cornflakes locked in the living room, and left for good, despite Re'ach's frenzied barking.

Why was she so insecure? The vet thought because she was the runt of the litter but I wondered if she'd caught it from me – because at that time any disapproval sent me into depression. I remember being cold-shouldered by some snob social group, perhaps because I was Jewish, perhaps because I was just me. Anyway it hurt.

Help came from an unexpected source – an old Maltese woman, who used to stand beside me at the village bus stop. She used to detail all her difficulties to God, whom she located in the wayside shrine close by. From her nods, she seemed to receive answers, so I tried God too. His answer came more promptly than I expected, for a thought from Marx, Groucho not Karl, surfaced in my mind before I could say Amen.

"Any club that accepted him he didn't care to be a member of." I never thought eternity had such a sense of humour.

In prayer I also got more serious advice. He taught me that people only dislike in you what they hate in themselves, so don't make devils of people you don't get on with.

Also everybody is somebody's least favourite person – which is unpleasant but good for you like strong greens, ugly winter undies and cod liver oil. We all exist to rub away each other's vanity.

But even the loss of vanity can hurt like hell especially if you're the over-sensitive type. So here's a practical suggestion if you're the shy type and dreading those awful office parties. Have a pray before the party. This isn't just pious, it's practical. Remembering eternity really helps you not to take this world and its popularity too much to heart, nor its fashions too seriously.

LB

Lionel's mention of not joining a club that would have someone like him as a member brought to mind this poem by Delmore Schwartz. Born in Brooklyn, he was a leading figure in literary-political circles in the thirties and forties. His poetry and short stories explored the alienation of modern people and traced the experiences of Jews coming to America as immigrants and the fate of their children.

Shyness and disapproval

THE WOULD-BE HUNGARIAN

Come, let us meditate upon the fate of a little boy who
    wished to be
Hungarian! Having been moved with his family to a
    new suburb, having been sent to a new school, the
    only Catholic school in the new suburb
Where all the other children were Hungarian,

He felt very sad and separate on the first day, he felt
    more and more separated and isolated
Because all the other boys and girls pitied and were
    sorry for him since he was not
Hungarian! Hence they pitied and were sorry for him
    so much they gave him handsome gifts,
Presents of comic books, marbles and foreign coins,
    peppermints and candy, a pistol, and also their
    devoted sympathy, pity and friendship

Making him sadder still since now he saw how all
    Hungarians were very kind and generous, and he
    was not

Hungarian! Hence he was an immigrant, an alien: he
    was and he would be,
Forever, no matter what, he could never become
    Hungarian!
Hungarian! Hence he went home on the first day,
    bearing his gifts and telling his parents how much he
    wished to be
Hungarian: in anguish, in anger,
Accusing them of depriving him, and misusing him:
    amusing them,
So that he rose to higher fury, shouting and accusing
    them

How to Get Up When Life Gets You Down

– Because of you I am a stranger, monster,
  orang-outang!
Because of you (his hot tears say) I am an orang-
  outang! and not
Hungarian! Worse than to have no bicycle, no shoes . . .
Behold how this poor boy, who wished so passionately
  to be Hungarian
Suffered and knew the fate of being American.
  Whether on Ellis Island, Plymouth Rock,

Or in the secret places of the mind and heart
This is America – as poetry and hope
This is the fame, the game and the names of our fate:
This we must suffer or must celebrate.
      Delmore Schwartz, *The Literature of American Jews*

JM

7

Saying sorry

I opened the post and found a letter inviting me back to Berlin. The last time I was there it was still two cities, two worlds really, and I've got one of the last visas issued by the GDR to cross to the East and visit the palace of Potsdam.

But I don't want to revisit Potsdam on this coming trip. I want to trot along to a corset shop instead, in what was the East. No, I'm not going there to wear one, but to view one – not because I'm kinky and into undies, but for, well, you could call it research.

There was this shabby shop in a grim granite block in a potholed street in East Berlin. In the window was one whaleboned corset. The bones were yellowing with age, like bad teeth, and the cloth was covered by fine grey dust.

But what fascinated me were the bright red propaganda ribbons and banners festooned around it. "Our republic cares for its workers" they said. And "We work for the people's future".

What would a worker of the future want with a grey-boned dingy belt with dangling rusty suspenders? The mind boggled.

Is the window still there I wonder? Do the banners still decorate those bare bones? This I must see and shall lose no time. It's been like that for the last twenty years. If it's gone, well I'll believe there's really a new ball game in Old Berlin.

It was quite absurd of course. But there was so much that was absurd in the people's paradise.

The ritual at the restaurant I used to lunch in never varied. A waiter in coat and tails handed me a long de luxe menu, at the same time recommending the German goulash or the Hungarian goulash. "I'll try the trout," I said, testing his defences.

"I'm sorry sir, it hasn't been delivered yet," he replied blandly.

"Well, I'll try the steak," I said.

"The chef who prepares it is away," he countered. "I suggest the German goulash or the Hungarian goulash. Sir," he added suavely. So sometimes I chose the German goulash and sometimes the Hungarian goulash. It was a game of the absurd because despite the menu there was never anything else available and both the German and the Hungarian goulash tasted exactly the same.

But what was not absurd were the people who gave their lives in the East to build the people's paradise. I met some of them, a girl who cycled across Europe in 1946 to return to the land that had rejected her and clean up the mess Hitler had left behind. I met a man who sacrificed comfort and prosperity in Canada, where he had built a new life, to return to the bare shops and endless restrictions of the Democratic Republic out of patriotism. They were great people, true idealists.

So, what went wrong? Well the experts will give you all sorts of reasons, economic, sociologic, dialectical and political. But as a non-expert I can only report what I saw. The Democratic Republic thought it was infallible.

It could never admit making a mistake. It could never say sorry and start again.

Lots of individuals are like that too. I used to deal with religious divorces for my organization. Marriages collapsed just like the East German state because both partners were too proud or stubborn to say "sorry" or "it's my fault" – so they could never start afresh.

Some students asked me what were the most godly words a person can utter. I think they expected some prayer or text from Scripture. Well, my suggestion wasn't "Almighty God" or "Oh Lord", it was "Sorry mate, my mistake, I'll move over", or "No, don't worry dear, it was all my fault."

Saying sorry is not a weakness, but a strength, provided you really mean it. It sounds simple, but it's harder than it seems, though ever efficacious. And this applies not only to people but to politics as well. For it not only renews relationships and preserves marriages, it even stops states from tottering.

If the German Democratic Republic had been able to say the same, I might still be tucking into my Hungarian or German goulash in a restaurant in East Berlin, watched over by a benign bust of Lenin. If the same simple words could be said in the Middle East today, how many innocent lives might yet be spared.

LB

8

"Your ways are not My ways, says God"

(ISAIAH 55:8)

Lionel and I were both entranced by this piece by the Italian writer Natalia Ginzburg. A good part of married life, or any long-term partnership, is made up of the tiny differences, irritations and frictions that she describes so well. The trick is learning how to live with them. The snag is that all too often we recognize the things our partner does that annoy us, but it is harder to recognize, or admit, how we can be as maddening in return.

When things go well we can cope; when they start to fall apart, these little irritations can get blown up into the murderous anger and bitterness of the divorce court.

A counsellor who works with couples whose marriages are falling apart reassures them at the first session. "At the end of this process you will all like your partners much more, because you will have explored and understood all the ways you irritate and hurt each other. You may not still be married! – but at least you will like each other."

It may seem a bit odd to introduce this piece with the quote from Isaiah. But if we believe that God has a permanent relationship with every human being, there has to be a similar sort of accommodation on both sides. Perhaps that is why so many clergy retrain as counsellors.

HE AND I

He always feels hot, I always feel cold. In the summer when it really is hot he does nothing but complain about how hot he feels. He is irritated if he sees me put a jumper on in the evening.

He speaks several languages well; I do not speak any well. He manages – in his own way – to speak even the languages that he doesn't know.

He has an excellent sense of direction, I have none at all. After one day in a foreign city he can move about in it as thoughtlessly as a butterfly. I get lost in my own city; I have to ask directions so that I can get back home again. He hates asking directions; when we go by car to a town we don't know he doesn't want to ask directions and tells me to look at the map. I don't know how to read maps and I get confused by all the little red circles and he loses his temper.

He loves the theatre, painting, music, especially music. I do not understand music at all, painting doesn't mean much to me, and I get bored at the theatre. I love and understand one thing in the world and that is poetry.

He loves museums, and I will go if I am forced to but with an unpleasant sense of effort and duty. He loves libraries and I hate them.

He loves travelling, unfamiliar foreign cities, restaurants. I would like to stay at home all the time and never move.

All the same I follow him on his many journeys. I follow him to museums, to churches, to the opera. I even follow him to concerts, where I fall asleep . . .

He is not shy; I am shy. Occasionally however I have seen him be shy. With the police when they come over to the car armed with a notebook and pencil. Then he is shy, thinking he is in the wrong.

And even when he doesn't think he is in the wrong. I think he has a respect for established authority. I am afraid of established authority, but he isn't. He respects it. There is a difference. When I see a policeman coming to fine me I immediately think he is going to haul me off to prison. He doesn't think about prison; but, out of respect, he becomes shy and polite . . .

Everything I do is done laboriously, with great difficulty and uncertainty. I am very lazy, and if I want to finish anything it is absolutely essential that I spend hours stretched out on the sofa. He is never idle, and is always doing something; when he goes to lie down in the afternoons he takes proofs to correct or a book full of notes; he wants us to go to the cinema, then to a reception, then to the theatre – all on the same day. In one day he succeeds in doing, and making me do, a mass of different things, and in meeting extremely diverse kinds of people. If I am alone and try to act as he does I get nothing at all done, because I get stuck all afternoon somewhere I had meant to stay for half an hour, or because I get lost and cannot find the right street, or because the most boring person and the one I least wanted to meet drags me off to the place I least wanted to go to.

If I tell him how my afternoon has turned out he says it is a completely wasted afternoon and is amused and makes fun of me and loses his temper; and he says that without him I am good for nothing.

I don't know how to manage my time; he does . . .

I don't know how to drive. If I suggest that I should get a licence too he disagrees. He says I would never manage it. I think he likes me to be dependent on him for some things . . .

I am very untidy. But as I have got older I have come to miss tidiness, and I sometimes furiously tidy up all the cupboards. I think this is because I remember my mother's tidiness. I rearrange the linen and blanket cupboards and in the summer I reline every drawer with strips of white cloth. I rarely rearrange my papers because my mother didn't write and had no papers. My tidiness and untidiness are full of complicated feelings of regret and sadness. His untidiness is triumphant. He has decided that it is proper and legitimate for a studious person like himself to have an untidy desk.

He does not help me get over my indecisiveness, or the way I hesitate before doing anything, or my sense of guilt. He tends to make fun of every tiny thing I do. If I go shopping in the market he follows me and spies on me. He makes fun of the way I shop, of the way I weigh the oranges in my hand unerringly choosing, he says, the worst in the whole market; he ridicules me for spending an hour over the shopping, buying onions at one stall, celery at another and fruit at another. Sometimes he does the shopping to show me how quickly he can do it; he unhesitatingly buys everything from one stall and then manages to get the basket delivered to the house. He doesn't buy celery because he cannot abide it.

And so – more than ever – I feel I do everything inadequately or mistakenly. But if I once find out that he has made a mistake I tell him so over and over again until he is exasperated. I can be very annoying at times.

His rages are unpredictable, and bubble over like the head on beer. My rages are unpredictable too, but his quickly disappear whereas mine leave a noisy nagging trail behind them which must be very annoying – like the complaining yowl of a cat.

Sometimes in the midst of his rage I start to cry, and instead of quieting him down and making him feel sorry for me this infuriates him all the more. He says my tears are just play-acting, and perhaps he is right. Because in the middle of my tears and his rage I am completely calm.

I never cry when I am really unhappy . . .

About twenty years ago when I first knew him . . . I remember that one evening he walked me back to the *pensione* where I was living; we walked together along the *Via Nazionale*. I already felt that I was very old and had been through a great deal and had made many mistakes, and he seemed a boy to me, light years away from me . . . If I remind him of that walk along the *Via Nazionale* he says he remembers it, but I know he is lying and that he remembers nothing: and I sometimes ask myself if it was us, these two people, almost twenty years ago on the *Via Nazionale*; two people who conversed so politely, so urbanely, as the sun was setting; who chatted a little about everything perhaps and about nothing; two friends talking, two young intellectuals out for a walk; so young, so educated, so uninvolved, so ready to judge one another with kind impartiality; so ready to say good-bye to one another for ever, as the sun set, at the corner of the street.

Natalia Ginzburg, "He and I" from *The Little Virtues*

JM

9

Not recognizing your own happiness

What do I think of my fellow clergymen?

Quite a lot! They're long-suffering, pious, unselfish in patches and self-absorbed. Their self-absorption is the cause of their absentmindedness.

Take the late Reverend Baring Gould, vicar of a church I used to visit in Essex. After a confirmation service, he bent down benignly to a little boy and enquired kindly, "And whose child are you?"

"Yours, father," sobbed the boy.

And I recall some nice nuns, who out of charity sold off some land for a sports centre. They remembered just in time the grave of their reverend mother, positioned in front of the goal posts.

And here's a fragment of conversation I overheard at a synagogue conference. A woman surged up to a scholarly continental rabbi, who had once awarded her a study diploma. "Oh Rabbi," she breathed, "you sat on my board."

"Madam, I sat on your vot?" he replied indignantly.

Well, it's a giggle for our congregations, who can forgive our failure to see the obvious, provided we can point out what isn't so obvious – the signs of God's love in a world sick with loneliness and longing.

I hesitantly offer two practical pointers, and hope they're helpful.

Firstly, I think there's more love on offer than we realize, but we don't let ourselves see it. I knew a girl who longed for love. It took her twenty years to realize it was there, waiting for her, because her chap didn't come on a white charger, but by bus. And it was much the same with me too. Looking back on my own life, I see now the love I yearned for was offered me many times, but I rejected it, or didn't even see it, because it wasn't packaged in the way I expected.

The second pointer is this. Often the key to what you want is given you, but you can't or won't recognize it. I too longed for human love, but could only achieve the divine sort. It's called sublimation, and it made me mad. Later on I realized it's right to learn to love God before you experiment on your fellow human beings.

These thoughts came into my mind last week after a fellow rabbi told me this odd story about a man who wandered through a desert parched with thirst. Suddenly he saw another man and staggered towards him. "Water, water!" he cried.

"I can't give you a drink," said the other, "but I can get you a dinner jacket."

The man staggered on bemused, and then saw another wayfarer in the wilderness.

"Water, a drink!" he begged.

"Sorry, old boy, I can't give you a drink, only a dinner jacket!"

The man staggered on yet again, until he saw a hotel in the desert with a bar, and it wasn't a mirage. "Give me a drink!" he croaked to the doorman.

"But, sir," said the doorman, "I can't let you in without a dinner jacket."

Now some said it was a silly story. I thought it said a lot about life and love. Perhaps it has a message for you. Perhaps God has already given you the key to what you pray for, but you don't yet recognize it. Seeing the obvious is surprisingly difficult, as any artist can tell you. It requires great experience, or great innocence. Sit back and consider afresh what is around you, what stares you in the face.

LB

10

Happy endings

Religious instruction, in my first school, was a turn-off. In school assembly we sang "All things bright and beautiful" and led by a teacher on a Franciscan kick, we thanked God for Sister Snowdrop, Brother Buttercup and other exotica in London's brick jungle.

But being streetwise Stepney kids, what about Brother Prejudice, Sister Dole Queue, and Auntie Cancer, who'd called on Grandma uninvited? Did we thank God for creating them too? But if you left them out, religion became like "Toytown", *Swallows and Amazons*, and kids with nannies in nurseries, like the Regency romances I read now when life gets too tough.

Years later, when I gingerly re-examined the Bible, I was pleasantly surprised to find life's unpleasant parts left in.

"Man is born into trouble as the sparks fly upward" (*Job 5:7*).
"In sin my mother conceived me" (*Psalm 51:5*).
"The day of one's death is better than the day of one's birth" (*Ecclesiastes 7:2*).

Not reassuring stuff but recognizable.

But something in us can't leave it like that. We demand happy endings, and millionaires make their millions providing them for us. That's what Westerns, musicals and TV soaps are about. I was told this anecdote about Billy Wilder whose wit made Hollywood sparkle. They say he went to see Sam Goldwyn with a project for a film on Nijinsky. "It's too downbeat, Billy," said Sam. "Sure he comes to the West, becomes a famous ballet dancer and packs them in, but look what happens afterwards – he goes mad. He thinks he's a horse!"

"Don't worry, Sam," said Billy. "We'll make sure he wins the Derby."

Well, that works fine in films, but what about real life? Can I provide the happy endings that have eluded saints and seers for centuries? Yes, but there's a hidden catch. The only way to get it is to give it, so it doesn't quite come for free! Though we can't supply happy endings for ourselves, we can provide happier endings for each other.

Look, there's a phone by your elbow. Ring up old so-and-so, you quarrelled with years ago, though you don't remember now who said what to whom or why. Now she or he might still quote your words back verbatim. Never mind. You can make a happier ending happen – you only risk a rebuff.

And though Auntie Cancer still visits uninvited, there's all the difference in the world between coming back after your chemo to a cold and empty bedsit, and someone coming to fetch you, and sitting you down with a kiss, a cuddle and a cuppa.

Now I could carry on to provide you with even happier endings, but the point is you've got to provide them yourself for someone else instead. That's the only way we'll all ever get one.

LB

Lionel isn't the only one who likes happy endings. This little song is by a Yiddish writer called I. Kotliar. I know no more about it than the little note that accompanies it in a German collection of Yiddish songs put together by Hai and Topsy Frankl. They record that it is based on an earlier version that was sung in many ghettos during the German occupation – so it became a plea for hope in a time of war and despair.

SCHPIL-SHE MIR A LIDELE IN JIDDISCH

Play me a little song in Yiddish,
one that brings joy
and no nasty surprises.

One that all people can understand,
great and small,
for it must go from mouth to mouth.
    Play, play, musicians
        you know already what I mean and what I want!
    Play, play me a song,
        play a tune with heart and feelings.

A song without sighing and tears.
Play it so that all can hear it,
so that all can see: I'm alive and I can still sing!
more sweetly and better than before.
    Play . . .

Play me the song of peace,
of true peace and not just a dream
that all peoples, great and small,
must understand each other
behave towards each other without war or strife.
    Play . . .

Let us sing, sing the song together,
like good friends, like children of one mother.
The only thing I desire
is that it ring out free and true,
a song that is my own and for all peoples.
    Play . . .

        From *Jiddische Lieder*, Hai and Topsy Frankl

JM

Only real religion will do

"How wonderful you've found faith, Lionel," says an eager, non-religious friend of mine who takes a romantic view of religion. "I can feel your inner peace."

"Yers, yers," I reply to spare his illusions. Poor fool, it's not *finding* faith that's difficult but keeping it and translating it into the practical details of daily life.

Here's an all too common spiritual scenario. You don't believe, but drop in to a place of worship. Perhaps you're curious, perhaps it's raining. You're startled when a cosy chat with the cosmos starts up and you bathe in peace like a jacuzzi. But before you get proprietorial about that peace, be warned, God has a habit of pulling it away from underneath you.

One day, for example, you return eagerly to the same place for a second chat. But this time the service falls flat as a pancake. God's gone and what remains is stodge. Lots of people give up religion at this point, because pressing on requires serious soul-searching. What are you into the God business for anyway? Raptures and tingles, or for awkward things, like the truth, duty and integrity you need to lead a decent life? As for inner peace, you get just enough doled out to do just that but no more, even though they say it's all waiting for you at the end when you've done life's homework. It's just the same with outer peace as the inner sort. I admire politicians and diplomats who fly from one fruitless committee to another, demonstrating for peace by trying to tie up its tiresome details – like pulling a tablecloth this way and that, to cover a table it doesn't fit. That's what religion's like too.

The religious greats like Wesley, St Teresa and the Jewish

mystics were caustic about religion which preferred raptures to the realities of life, and their practicality shocked their pious followers. This sad, sexist story illustrates the point.

A distraught father consults a great Jewish sage and mystic.

"Rabbi," he pleads, "I'm old and my daughter's so ugly no one will marry her. What will become of her?"

"But how ugly?" said the practical sage.

"If you put her beside a herring on a plate," sobbed the father, "you'd prefer the herring."

"What sort of herring?" asked the sage.

"Oy, oy, does such a detail matter?" wailed the nonplussed father. "A Dutch herring maybe, a salted one."

The sage pondered. "That's a pity," he said. "If it had been a pickled herring now, she might have had a hope."

Visions, warm feelings and moments of grace are not that rare. It's working them out in the details of daily life that's hard. That's the difference between sentimental religion and the real thing. The former is suitable for self-indulgent moods. Only the latter will serve for real pain and suffering.

LB

12

Suburban barbecues
and starving babies

Summer is a-coming in and suburbia celebrates Texan-style with blazing barbecues, fired by charcoal brickettes. "It's all happening," says my mother excitedly and bullies me into taking her along.

Smoke gets in your eyes, as the lovely old song says. So does a chip off the old charcoal. I can't converse, so while my mother socializes I sit in sullen meditation with one eye closed and the other rimmed with red.

But you need both eyes about you at a barbecue. You can tell by feel which side your baguette is buttered, but you need your eyes to know which side of your chop is burnt and which is bloody.

With one eye, I see a cook has set fire to his pinny. I hear his squeals but feel no sympathy, for there is a whiff of meths from the meal. Next time I shall bring a compass to tell me which way the wind blows.

It is, alas, blowing my way now, reeking of sausage fat. But there is a recession, so they can only set cheap chipolatas alight, not whole oxen or heifers. I suddenly wonder what the animal sacrifices were like that the Bible describes in the Sinai desert – I think of all that gore in all that heat and I shudder.

But I admire the ancient Hebrews. They were refugees like the Kurds and Somalis now, and destitute like the Bangladeshis, and the animals they sacrificed were their only wealth. They knew what we moderns don't want to know – that religion isn't real without sacrifice. Could I watch my savings go up in smoke? I doubt it.

Now this touches my sore spot. I saw a picture in a paper of a starving kid you could keep alive for a few pounds. I feel manipulated but I can't get it out of my mind. I have to give to keep my religious self-respect.

But how much? How long is a piece of string? I know I'm not going to give everything to the poor – but nor are you.

One day by a miracle I might, but I wouldn't bank on it. I think back again to the Bible, for a rabbi said God didn't give His revelation to angels. It was meant for fallible human beings like us. So why not give the tithe of my income, commanded in that revelation, to charity? It may make the problem manageable, helping the starving Third World babies, and me.

Ten per cent net isn't heroic but if you're no saint like me, yet still have a conscience, there's a lot to recommend it – it's biblically-based and practical, provided you keep it up.

One of my hosts interrupts my meditation to offer me more burnt flesh. I politely decline. When I get home, after I've sent my cheque, I shall reward my modest contribution to charity with a modest nut cutlet, cooked medium rare in a microwave. With baked beans and brown sauce it's yummy.

The Talmud wisely says, "Just because you can't finish the job, isn't an excuse for not doing something about it."

LB

13

Making it big in the next life

I stood outside a pie shop frowning and waiting to be inter-viewed for an outside broadcast on London market life. Something deep down was bugging my memory, but what?

Yes, I certainly remembered trying to make a pie myself once. I mixed the dough according to the instructions, and tried to roll it out with a milk bottle, which drove me frantic, for it kept shredding into lace. I tried to repair the holes by gluing them first with water and then with spittle, until the pastry got as grey as I felt. And in a burst of temper, I threw the grisly lump through the window, where it hit my dog who howled. The recipe never told me about flouring the pastry board. Now there was no beauti-ful thought in that.

And then I still sometimes indulge in a childhood fantasy of being locked up in a pie shop overnight. I'd nibble a bit of crust here and try a filling there, till I collapsed, gorged but happy, to greet the dawn with a bump, which is not a very beautiful thought either.

And then it hit me. A pie shop in a market, that's where my father taught me the facts of life, or tried to, for I was only five at the time. This is how it happened.

In the great depression my family fell on hard times. My father was an out-of-work master tailor. He and my mother tried their hand at a sweet shop but my father was no businessman, he was far too generous. He gave away most of the stock, and my mother ate the rest. Which is how he came to be in an East London market selling ice cream in the depths of winter. He sat me in a nearby jellied eel and pie shop. It was warm and through the window he kept an eye on me, while I kept two fascinated eyes on two mangy dogs, one of whom was mounting the other.

Now I hand it to my father, he didn't dodge the issue, unlike the nanny of an upper-class friend of mine. When he was faced with the same sight, she told him one poor doggy was ill, dear, and the other was a doggy VAD nurse, who was wheeling it to hospital.

This would have certainly sounded more plausible than the things my embarrassed father tried to tell me, which I thought more fanciful than any fairy story and far more horrible.

Suddenly he stared at the two exhausted dogs, stopped and bolted out of the shop. He returned with one decrepit pooch, covered with suppurating sores. My father demanded a pail of water, carbolic soap and disinfectant, which he got because he was a big man and a boxer. Then to the consternation of the management and undeterred by the cries and complaints of the customers, whose appetites he was spoiling, he washed the dog in the doorway all over, fondling it and feeding it his own jellied eels.

I cringed with embarrassment and tried to apologize for him. But then a beefy market man, who was one of the loudest complainers, turned to me and said, "Don't apologize for your dad, boy! He makes us mad, but you might not know it, he's a saint!"

Which shut me up sharply! Even if my father turned out to be no tycoon in this world, he might make it big in the next. He certainly failed to teach me the facts of life. I found out those later by trial and error, with more of the latter than the former, alas. But I did learn what goodness is like, which is a fact of eternal life. It was a fair swap.

Anyway, that's what bugged my memory as I stood frowning while I waited by a pie shop in a market.

LB

II
Catastrophes and Disasters

14

The way God sees it

To my surprise I worked out a religious talk in record time. There was a beginning and ending, a joke which hadn't been heard too many times before, and of course a dollop of uplift for God. Now I'd even have spare time, I told myself happily, to go to a caff, munch a coconut slice and read my newspaper.

But I hadn't reckoned with the old spoilsport on high. "It won't do, Lionel," said His voice inside me.

"Why won't it do?" I said out loud belligerently, frightening a lady nearby who transferred herself and her Eccles cake to another table fast.

"Because it isn't what I want," and then there was the usual obstinate silence.

Though most worshippers won't admit it, religion would be much easier if God didn't interfere so much. For instance, just as I'm blessing the food at a banquet and about to tuck in, He whispers to me, "What about the starving Somalis, Lionel?" and ruins my appetite. Or I'm giving a talk on the suffering of Jewish refugees and He adds, though no one else can hear, "Fine, and what about the poor Kurds, Cambodians and Palestinians?" and I don't know how to handle it.

Now if you want to keep God out of religion and lots of people do, even clerics, here's some professional advice how you do it.

One way is to turn God into a totem, of your own particular community, church or tribe. You can enjoy cheering Him, rooting for Him, and wearing all sorts of knick-knacks with His name on – like a football supporter. It looks pious, it feels pious. You only have to forget your

God is also God of the other side too.

You can also use liturgy to lock God out of religion. It's quite simple really. You say so many prayers so fast, that you've got no time to listen – so God can't get a word in edgeways. There's also so much kneeling, twirling, prostrating, bowing and bending backwards you've got no time to listen to His still small voice, even if the choirs haven't drowned it.

You can also trivialize God out of existence by taking His name in vain. Now taking God's name in vain is an old-fashioned problem, but it still makes me uncomfortable and I said so at a New York party when everyone was exclaiming, "My God this" or "my God that". "OK, Rabbi, what do we say?" they asked. So I told them about an old Archbishop who went to consecrate an unfinished church. As he processed through the door a workman hit himself with a hammer and shouted, "Nom de Dieu!". "Don't be a blasphemer, my son," said the Cardinal Archbishop kindly, as he processed by. "Why don't you say 'merde' like everybody else?"

Munching my coconut slice, an odd thought came to me. What does God make of our religion? I suddenly felt sorry for Him. How does He endure all our nagging prayers, our manipulative promises, all that shmaltzy flattery. What do we and our religion look like from His point of view? Actually it's not too difficult to find out.

Do sit back, and ask God to show you how your life looks in His eyes, not your own, or your friends', or your family's, or your neighbours'. Don't go into orgies of guilt. You might get a surprise. He might think your failures a success or vice versa of course.

You might save yourself a lot of misery if you look at your life from the standpoint of eternity.

LB

15

The "beyond life"

The moment my mother wakes up, she leaps into her clothes and is off like a bullet to her friendly caff. Licking a double ice in the window, she cheers on young lovers, O.A.Ps and cursing car drivers. She loves life.

Meanwhile my aunt methodically completes her *maquillage*. It takes her two hours, sometimes three. But when she proceeds to her patisserie, where the waitresses wear lace pinnies, the result is perfect. The sisters eye each other with amused affection from a distance.

But alas no longer, for my aunt has been taken to hospital and my mother mopes. My aunt is trying not to mope but finds it hard. The staff are kind but she is surprised to find herself in a ward of old women, because she does not consider herself such. Her world has grown old with her so she has not noticed.

I try to wheedle a joke out of her, because for such a proper lady she has quite an improper sense of humour, but she is too weak and the indignity of her body is beyond a joke. I hold her hand as she goes to sleep, looking like the little girl she once was. She'll get by, I tell myself, she'll cope, because she has inner resources. Her religion is unsentimental, but solid.

My mother is now all for afterlife, convinced her own mother's waiting to clasp her on the other side. She may be right! But my aunt adds – what about my grandfather? – heaven knows what he'll be like without his whisky. Nectar was never his line.

My aunt should know. After my grandmother died, she looked after my grandfather and all the children, caring for a younger sister who lost her lung in the sweatshops, and nursing a dying brother through the blitz. Though cautious about afterlife, my aunt has no such hesitations about "beyond life". The strength she needed never came from this world, nor did her sense of duty and decency. That "beyond life" that bore her up then will steady her now among the oldies.

Now what is happening to my aunt will also happen to you and me if we're lucky enough to reach ninety. And I give you this advice. Make friends with that "beyond life" before you need its strength, not after, before you end up in a hospital, retirement home or hospice. Good deeds done for its sake will bring it closer, so will minutes of quietness in places of prayer. It's useful even now. That "beyond life" will support you in every crisis – in a geriatric ward, or a hospice. It's what keeps people decent even in a hostage hideout in the Middle East.

LB

16

Where does suffering come from?

There are plenty of problems in the world that can make us suffer. So it seems very unfair that we can also be ambushed from inside ourselves as well. Sad moods that tip over into depression are the "clinical" end of this. But as well as outer disasters and inner illnesses we have more than enough personal ways of making ourselves miserable.

Sometimes people who have lived in extreme situations can remind us of just how much harm we can do to ourselves. For years the Jewish world petitioned the Soviet authorities for the release of Anatholy Sharansky, one of the leading "refuseniks", Russian Jews who had sought permission to leave Russia and join their families in Israel. Once someone had applied and been "refused" permission, they automatically lost their jobs and then ran the risk of further harassment as "parasites". Sharansky was arrested as one of the members of the Helsinki Committee that monitored Human Rights abuses in the Soviet Union, and he spent years in the gulag. In his memoirs he talks about the need for facing the reality of the situation in which we find ourselves.

> During these years I have met people who have been weakened from constant disappointments. They continually create new hopes for themselves, and as a result they betray themselves. Others live in the world of illusions, hastily and incessantly building and rebuilding their world in order to prevent real life from ultimately destroying it.
>
> What then is the solution? The only answer is to find the meaning of your current life. It's best if you are left with only one hope – the hope of remaining yourself no matter what happens.

Don't fear, don't believe, and don't hope. Don't believe words from the outside; believe your own heart. Believe in that meaning which was revealed to you in this life, and hope that you will succeed in guarding it.

Elsewhere he notes: "Nothing they can do can humiliate me. I can only humiliate myself."
Anatholy Sharansky, *Fear No Evil: A Memoir.*

The psychotherapist Viktor Frankl, himself a survivor of Auschwitz, also writes about the need to find meaning in our situation, however bad it may be.

Whenever one is confronted with an inescapable, unavoidable situation, whenever one has to face a fate which cannot be changed, e.g. an incurable disease, such as an incurable cancer; just then one is given a last chance to actualize the highest value, to fulfil the deepest meaning, the meaning of suffering. For what matters above all is the attitude we take toward suffering, the attitude in which we take our suffering upon ourselves.

Let me cite a clear-cut example: once, an elderly general practitioner consulted me because of his severe depression. He could not overcome the loss of his wife who had died two years before and whom he had loved above all else. Now how could I help him? What should I tell him? Well, I refrained from telling him anything but instead confronted him with the question, "What would have happened, Doctor, if you had died first, and your wife would have had to survive you?"

"Oh," he said, "for her this would have been terrible; how she would have suffered!"

Whereupon I replied, "You see, Doctor, such a suffering has been spared her, and it was you who have spared her this suffering; but now, you have to pay for it by surviving and mourning her." He said no word but shook my hand and calmly left my office. Suffering ceases to be suffering in some way at the moment it finds a meaning, such as the meaning of a sacrifice.
Victor Frankl, *Man's Search for Meaning*

Where does suffering come from?

Perhaps our psychological distress hides a deeper spiritual crisis. Rabbi Abraham Isaac Kook was the first Chief Rabbi of Palestine this century. A mystic, his writings are not easy to understand, but here he tries to discover the inner life of the soul behind the melancholy that each of us may experience.

One needs to determine clearly the nature of that intangible something pressing on his heart, saddening and embittering his life, for which there seems to be no conscious explanation. In most instances, when some reason for this mood is sought, only a surface explanation is attained, the truth being much deeper than all that can be grasped or understood by the clear mental processes.

But the fact is that this melancholy of the spirit is the very substance of the soul's singing. It is the soul asking its freedom, wrestling with that which presses upon it, reaching out for a life of freedom, a life higher and finer, clearer and brighter . . .

Therefore it is proper and necessary to analyse and to take advantage as much as possible of this mood of the soul, to lift pearls out of murky depths – to distill from them exquisite emotions. For after all, in whatever manner, and wherever a person's soul makes itself evident, there is evidence of the beginning of deliverance; the light of salvation pushing to reveal itself from behind the blackness.

> Herbert Weiner from Proceedings of the
> Central Conference of American Rabbis, 1964

The same idea was put more graphically by the German poetess Mascha Kaleko:

> When the waves break over me
> I dive down deep and look for pearls.

JM

17

The incomplete world

You wake up on a Monday morning, pick up the newspaper, switch on the radio, and wonder what sort of world you're in. You've got your own personal problems – there's the tax form falling through the letter box and an awkward interview with your boss, and there's no marge left in the fridge. You feel gruff and growly already. And when you turn on the radio, you shoot bolt upright and whimper because there's been another plane disaster – this time on a route you've flown on many times – death is very close. You need a cup of tea fast.

Some people say God is everywhere and in everything, so evil doesn't really exist. It's just good in disguise. We can't see it, that's all. I once tried to see the world that way and it made me cross-eyed. Neither concentration camps nor plane disasters are good in disguise. Dead bodies, weeping relatives are never good.

Some people take the opposite line and say if hell exists, then this is it. But that doesn't fit the facts either.

I meet too much goodness and love in this world for that – too much charity, too much kindness.

I think things go wrong and disasters happen because the world is an incomplete sort of place. Like you and me, it's struggling towards its own perfection, but it hasn't got there. It's still going through its birth pangs.

So what's our place in it? Well I once sat in a church not far from a concentration camp, and thought about all the tragedies that had happened there. "Why, God, didn't you take a hand in it?" I cried. Then I thought – how can God have hands? – He's pure spirit. But if He hasn't got hands, is He any use? Then suddenly it hit me. We're God's hands in the world and He works through us to complete His creation.

So don't dive back under your duvet as you read the news. Religion means facing facts not fleeing from them. Get up quickly, have your cup of tea, and work out what you can do. Can you comfort someone on the plane, or give something to a disaster fund? Monday morning can be dreadful – that's true, but that's why you're here. You might look and feel a mess but you're God's representative – His hands on earth, working to complete His creation.

It's what we were created for. So let's get up, and get on with it.

LB

There is a powerful echo of this idea that we must grasp hold of life despite tragedy in the classic book *When bad things happen to good people* by Harold S. Kushner, composed after the death of his young son who had been ill throughout his life. Less well known is a little collection called *Reflections in a Pumpkin Field* by Rabbi Jay R. Brickman. This collection of musings on life is also related to the tragic death of his son.

Several of our friends have commented on how well Rita and I seem to be bearing the loss of our beloved son, and I thought it might be of help to others to know some of the thoughts which crowd our minds in these difficult hours.

I find little consolation in the notion of a heavenly Kingdom where our souls will meet, though I do not dismiss such an event as being beyond possibility. Nor do I derive comfort from the belief that God so loved Andy that He drew our son to Himself. I find no meaning in this tragedy and this is perhaps the only comfort. Were I to believe there was justice in such an affliction, even a justice I do not understand, I think it would drive me mad.

An event such as this happens by chance, because death is as much part of the divine scheme as life. Sorrow is as intrinsic to human existence as joy.

It is neither philosophic acumen nor intensity of faith which enables us to keep functioning. Rather it is the life force which continues to assert itself within us. Friendship, fresh adventure, laughter are extremely important now. The miracle of Jewish survival in the face of the many horrors which have dogged us through the centuries was an appetite for life under almost any conditions. It is this same craving for existence which makes Rita and me wish to continue, and allows us to relish the days and experiences and friendships we may yet be privileged to know.

Jay R. Brickman, *Reflections in a Pumpkin Field.*

JM

18

Sod's Law

At the conference we compared notes about our childhood. I'd been born in London, and he in pre-war Poland, which was bad news for a Jewish child. But he was here, he'd survived.

"Your parents must have been pretty clever."

"No," he said thoughtfully, "not clever, just naïve. When the Germans invaded from the west in 1939, they fled east, and found themselves in the Russian zone. The Russians then asked the refugees if they wanted to return to their homes in the German zone, and my family were so homesick they said yes."

"So, how did you survive?"

"Ah," he said, "it was a trap. The Russians wanted to find out who was unreliable. My parents fell into it and we were deported to Siberia."

"How dreadful!"

"Not really," he said. "After we were deported, the Germans invaded Russia, but we were in such a God-forsaken corner of the country, no army ever came our way. That's how we survived. It's the case of Sod's Law in reverse."

I dare to quote this conversation, because Sod's Law is now ensconced in the latest edition of the Oxford English Dictionary, which relates it to Murphy's Law, which defines the apparent perverseness and unreasonableness of things – why for example the phone rings, just after you've soaped yourself in the bath, or why your toast always falls marmalade side down, or why Arsenal always score a goal on the box, as soon as you've gone off to make a cuppa.

I suffer from it most on solemn occasions. At the

cemetery, I lead the cortege behind the coffin to the grave, only to find they haven't dug it, and I have to tell everyone to come back at tea time. Or just when I've cooked five fish some fancy way, a guest turns up with his new fiancée and her former boyfriend, and not even a computer can divide five small soles into seven.

But Sod's Law wins out against all of us in the end, for death is so perverse. We all ask, "Why me, why now?" It's a real test of faith when you're brought up sharp against Sod's Law – whether it's comic like a ruined dinner or tragic like a terminal illness. If you can say, "I might make something out of that mess" or "perhaps there's even some goodness hidden in hell", then your faith is stronger than Sod's Law.

Now at first sight, Sod's Law seems reasonable and faith does not. So why am I for faith? Like much in religion, the evidence is slight but sufficient. All the people I know who've followed their faith, have not been made foolish by it, or ever seemed silly to me. On the contrary, because they believe beyond reason, I become more sane and courageous. I can live with more confidence because their belief is strong enough to say to Sod's Law, "Clear off!"

LB

19

Financial disaster

The details don't matter too much. We inherited some family money, were out of our depth and got involved with a business in trouble. As a result, we had to plough in a bit more to "save" it, and then more and more till we lost the lot.

It was a painful and shocking experience. I learnt for the first time how vulnerable I am, something that came as a shock to my previously comfortable middle-class experience. But I survived somehow, and in looking back it may be helpful to chart some of the problems and some of the solutions.

A. LIMITING THE DAMAGE

When everything was falling apart, we found ourselves a young solicitor who brought us down to the new reality: Forget the trimmings and the fantasies, what is the bottom line of what you have to preserve for the sake of survival, for you and your family? In our case it was the family home and the ability to carry on working – all the rest was really superfluous.

We learnt that you have to become starkly realistic about the extent of what you have lost, accept it, and emotionally say goodbye to it. Not easy to do at the best of times, but when everything seems to be running downhill out of control, you have to try to fix an objective, the minimum that must be salvaged, and then every strategy has to be geared to achieving that end. Including knowing when to fight, when to give up and when to settle, however unfair or unjust it may seem to you. At the time it feels totally unacceptable. In retrospect, if you survive, apart from the remaining resentment and hurt, you can learn to count your blessings. The great medieval Jewish scholar Maimonides put it pretty bluntly: "The things we really need are very few. The things we don't need are infinite, so our desire for them is infinite." It is the most obvious truth and one of the hardest things to learn.

B. COPING WITH THE ANGER

Anger has to go somewhere. If you don't let it out, it will boomerang back on you – it is one of the underlying factors of clinical depression. But sometimes anger is proportionate to your own awareness of having done something terribly stupid. When we first got the money, we became deliciously extravagant. At least in our fantasy – we lost most of the money before we had a chance to spend it! But all sorts of grandiose absurdities came creeping in. How to invest it so as to get additional money – off-shore islands, tax havens, business perks, second homes in exotic places. So when it all fell apart it was not reality that was lost, but all those dreams – so our anger was as great as our previous greed.

There is a story of a man who saw a newspaper headline that he had won one million pounds in the pools. When the cheque arrived it turned out that the newspaper had added a nought to the figure by mistake. So he spent the rest of his life bewailing the nine hundred thousand pounds he had lost.

But where do you put the anger – if you don't want to take it out on your family, friends or the cat (satisfactory in the short term, but it takes an awful lot of repair afterwards – though cats, I understand, are more forgiving). Without sounding too pious, I knew that I had to give it to God to deal with. But that is not so easy. In the short term you might as well have a blazing row, provided your theology allows it. You can sometimes cheat a bit by generalizing and tossing in some self-righteous anger about natural disasters, unfair deaths, human suffering etc., but it is healthier to be more precise about your own particular grievance.

C. THE BACK WAY OUT

At the height of the crisis, when it looked as if we would lose everything, money, home, job, self-respect, I thought about "ending it all". I would wake early in the morning after a restless night, my mind racing with all the disastrous possibilities, the hopelessness, the next deadline for some grotesque decision or event to take place. And suicide seemed a very comforting alternative option.

At the end of the day, it was not ignorance of a foolproof (and comfortable) method that stopped me. Perhaps it was a sort of innate desire for life, mixed with a religious sense that this was a test sent by God which had to be endured. On the surface, though, it was that good old anger. I was bloody well not going to lose my life as well as everything else!

All the material things I feared losing still did not amount to much when I measured them against family and friends, the value of my own life. It was all too silly! But better to have admitted the temptation and thought it through than to pretend that it was never there in the first place. That way lies suicide of the spirit which is much worse.

JM

20

Failure

A letter invites me to America to lecture on spirituality and I ring around my friends to make sure they know. They rightly consider such vainglory unbecoming in a contemplative. "No one's heard of you over there, so no one may come."

I am wondering whether to pack my expensive suit from the charity shop or my cheap suit from a real shop, when the telephone rings. A Christian American friend hesitatingly says, "No one's heard of you over here. Don't expect big numbers!" "Do numbers matter?" My friend sighs into the phone, so I assume they do.

My mother then shouts that there's another transatlantic call. "You're not known here, Lionel," says a rabbi and in chorus we say, "Don't worry if no one shows up." "My," says the rabbi surprised, "you're quick!"

On the plane over, I ponder these dire warnings. But when I arrive, I learn they're meant kindly. Over there, religion too is judged by results, so clergymen receive generous salaries and short contracts, and not even contemplatives can afford failure.

But all is well. Contemplation is "in", and people do come, and I wonder whether to remain in America. "You wouldn't make it," says an American friend kindly. "You're so messy." I flare up but he means my suit not my morals. "Over here you can't afford to look a failure!"

On the flight back to London, I remember I'm returning to a failure – the biggest booboo I ever made in broadcasting, not even excepting the confusion over a pork paté on a cookery programme.

On the day I left for America, I turned the first page of

my script in a studio and gaped – there was no second.

A lot of letters about this await me at home. "How did you feel?" asks one lady.

"Like a diver who realizes a moment too late, they've drained the pool."

Another lady writes, "I'd always wondered if Jews were too clever – you reassured me!" If we'd been that clever, madame, our history wouldn't be so tragic.

A gentleman says, "I never believed it was a live broadcast, till you messed it up – thank you."

Many people say, "Because you make mistakes, my own are easier to accept," and I'm touched.

Those letters taught me a lot. Though being spiritual doesn't relieve you of responsibility for checking pages, your true C.V. has to include some failure. Without it you can become clever, but never wise. Also, that you can't be certain about failure or success however hard you work – for God alone owns the result, and knows its place in His divine plan.

LB

21

Facing the suffering of others

Facing our own suffering is one thing, facing that of others is altogether different – either because we cannot (or do not want to) feel what they are going through, or because we are too deeply drawn into their situation and feel all the more helpless. And in their pain we have to face a reality that we may one day encounter ourselves.

This poem is by the American poet Aaron Kramer, whose work I discovered in the usual way – a volume of collected writings caught my eye in a shop for remaindered books ten years after publication.

ADVENTURE

Being operated on for the first time at forty-five
was one of my adventures.
Ordered to remove all dentures,
I laughed; wheeled in on a stretcher, I smiled –
knowing that I would be wheeled out alive;
that, compared to certain others, I had the health of a
    child.

For several days, since harvesting notes
is one of my professions,
I let myself swarm with anecdotes
and impressions
so that I could feel genuinely richer coming out,
despite the bill, than I had been
when going in.

Facing the suffering of others

There was, it is true, some pain to grumble about,
and for a while I was forbidden to drive,
but all in all
being operated on for the first time at forty-five
was what you might call a ball.

It was what you might call a ball, except
for the undertone, usually at night, that crept
in through the slats of the door
from other rooms along my floor
whose occupants were mostly older
than forty-five (though one of them was scarcely half),
and had been opened in more important places
than the left shoulder,
and did not laugh,
about dentures, and had no smiles on their faces,
so pale, so thin,
when the stretchers wheeled them in.

                    Aaron Kramer, *Poems and Other Writings* (*1940–1980*)

In my brief medical career (a year's house jobs and an unexpected week in the delivery room at Hadassah Hospital in
Jerusalem during the Six Day War) it was this sense of helplessness at other people's suffering that seems to have affec-
ted me most – certainly as is reflected in some of the poems I
wrote at the time.

My barber's wife died three weeks ago.
He told me awkwardly
fumbling with the scissors,
sorry to inject tiresome reality
into our haircut chat.
I mumbled helplessly about "suddenness".
"No," he said,
"she had a breast off three years ago
at your hospital."

He removed a paper bag from the shelf.
"Bread!
Do my own shopping now.
Better hide it,
someone might want a haircut and sandwich!"

We groped through vacant moments:
his daughter,
relations who would help,
her last days in a ward for incurables.
He watched me in the mirror
with eyes I could not understand,
our teasing familiarity
no preparation
for death.

Wearing a white coat on the wards gave me a curious status, even as a medical student. I had an authority I hardly deserved in my early twenties, but it was also a form of protection from too great a personal involvement. I might have come to terms with it in time if I hadn't moved into the rabbinate instead, but there was always an uneasy feeling of inadequacy – to be touching such intimate aspects of people's lives and be so uninvolved.

Perhaps the hardest thing was accepting the fact that someone I was treating was actually dying a slow lingering death. This was before the remarkable work of Dame Cicely Saunders and the Hospice movement in helping patient and staff alike to face the reality of death and thus becoming empowered to work together to ease the end.

She was dying and trying to tell me that she wanted to end it now. All she could do was repeat, "You know what I want you to do," and stare – but I was hardly able to hear or accept her words, let alone know what to do about it. The registrar had fewer problems, perhaps it was already routine. The doses of painkiller were to be increased till they had the desired effect, and that was it. But of course it was not.

That time I had the excuse that neither my medical training nor my "role" gave me the responsibility to do more. But
a few years later, as a student rabbi, I found myself by the
bedside of a congregant, a woman I'd known quite well, now
also in the final weeks of her life. Her husband asked me to
visit her and I found myself utterly tongue-tied and
unprepared. So I sat there, exchanged a few banalities,
perhaps I had the courage to hold her hand – and left.

He phoned again a few days later. She was angry with me,
he told me, and could I go again. I turned for help to a newly
ordained Lionel. He suggested that I ask her if there was
anything she was afraid of – and that opened up at least the
beginnings of a conversation she wanted to have about
whether there was an afterlife in Jewish belief. I do not know
if my answers helped; there was no momentous change,
either for her or for me. She died a few days later. But at least
I had made a first step past my own fears and embarrassment
and all the other taboos and anxieties that transform a dying
person into something alien and unapproachable. I had crossed a barrier to reach another human being.

JM

22

When you're suffering, think small!

I learnt most about religion, not from books, but while visiting hospitals.

I remember a conversation with a patient in an AIDS ward. "I've had enough counselling, thank you," he said politely and sighed. "It's not that real unless you're in the same situation."

"Well, what do you need?" I asked.

"Help with little things," he said with unexpected passion, "like help in getting into a bath, or with the shopping or at the launderette. An occasional drive to the country would be heaven," he added wistfully.

"Why don't you ask?" I said. "They're not big things."

"That's what everybody tells you," he said. "Then they tell you to ring up social services, or contact the district nurse, who's already got too much on her hands. But in my condition it's the little things in life that make or break you."

He was right, and in future I won't talk so big but make tea more often.

Hospitals have taught me how much healing there is in little things. Holding a patient's hand without saying a word is worth more than a mountain of grapes or a monster box of chocolates. In the cancer ward I learnt that if you break up time into little bits, and live each one separately, you can cope with chemo and life much more easily. In the psychiatric department I learnt that cleaning shoes is a good therapy, so is tidying up a drawer, or matching socks or stockings. They're not too worrying, but they're jobs that need to be done and they ease you back into normal life.

I know it sounds odd, but because of all this, my God has

grown smaller too. In my prayers I don't use the image of a mighty, macho, father figure, bossing the universe. Instead I think of God as a small child I protect, a patient I can comfort, a being I can make a cup of tea for, a suffering servant – there are lots of those in hospital wards.

If God's gone dead in you, perhaps you're looking at Him in the wrong way. Why not try to think small? I no longer for example ask God to reveal to me the mysteries of His cosmos. I now ask for much less, some knowledge of my next small step ahead, and a little courage to take it – no more. Prayer works when you don't get greedy and treat God like a department store.

Hospitals are a good place for humour, which is not a luxury but a necessity when you're ill. And while considering little things, here's a hospital joke about one.

An elderly Jewish woman from Russia is re-united after many years with her son who has made it in the capitalist West. "Son," she said, "do you still keep kosher?"

"Oh, Mama," he said, "here we eat everything on the menu."

"But you still say your prayers, son, don't you?" she said bewildered.

"Mama, businessmen are too busy. If you want to get on, you just don't have time."

His mother paused in thought and then said desperately, "Tell me you're still circumcised?"

LB

23

Providing your own contentment

When you're getting on towards sixty-two, you can't help feeling restless, because life's landscape is changing fast, and you're heading for a different horizon. Now I don't know whether that horizon is going to be nice or nasty but I do know it's come closer lately.

No, I'm not complaining – sixty-two isn't bad. You don't have to prove yourself any more. What you've done, you've done, and the rest is gravy. The problem is time. If you're going to write a book, then you'd better get on with it. If you dream of a different life, then make it happen fast or wake up.

Which is why I seriously thought of making a bolt for it, and getting away from it all, when I crossed the Pennines on my way to a lecture. I'd get off the beaten track, find a cheap cottage in a Yorkshire dale, forget London, the rubbish and the rat race, and settle down to silence, simplicity and contemplation – which is a piece of pathetic twaddle!

A friend of mine had the same dream. She exchanged her cosy metropolitan flat for a lonely country croft with only sheep for company. When I visited her, she couldn't stop talking – she went on and on and on. And the same would happen to me.

If you make a break for it, you can ditch your furniture, even your friends, but there's one thing you can't ditch – yourself. Where you go, your discontent goes with you. Now life's tough, and lots of us daydream to cushion the shock. After all daydreams don't make you drowsy like tranquillizers, or fat like comfort food. But they do have a hidden danger because they deceive you. They tell you that your problems and the solutions to those problems are outside you. Some of them may be – but most of them aren't.

Take holidays for example! If you're drooling over the travel brochure like me, remember the contentment you crave isn't in the weather or the hotel furnishings, it's inside you, waiting for you to discover it. So sit silently for a few minutes in the airport chapel or at an empty table in the departure lounge, search inside yourself and locate the happiness you're looking for in your own heart. If you do, you'll have a much better time. You'll relax, be less demanding, and make more friends.

If you get too desperate, you don't get what you want. Take the case of the envious Jewish mother at a friend's daughter's wedding. "Get me a doctor!" she cries as she faints to the floor. A young man rushes forward and bends over her. "Doctor", she says determinedly, "have I got a lovely girl for you." Is it any wonder her poor daughter is still single?

LB

Lionel's "cottage in the country" also sounds like a prison to me – I'm incurably urban. But it does seem to be the spirit with which you view things that matters. I heard a story once about a monk who visited someone in a nearby prison. He and the inmate swopped experiences. Both were confined inside a closed community with almost no opportunity to leave. Both suffered from the same institutional restraints and food. If anything the monk had fewer outside contacts than the prisoner. But one was there as an involuntary guest of the State and the other had chosen it as a vocation. According to the version I heard, the prisoner got a totally new perception of his situation and became quite religious. It is not recorded what happened to the monk.

But we do have the record of a remarkable woman, Rosa Luxemburg, who was a leading figure in the international Socialist movement in Europe in the first two decades of this century. She was a founder member of the German Communist Party, but was very critical of the Bolshevik reign of terror in the Soviet Union. She was imprisoned several times for her political views, the last time in Berlin in January 1919. On her way to prison she and her companion Karl Liebknecht were murdered.

This is my *third* Christmas under lock and key, but you needn't take it to heart. I am as tranquil and cheerful as ever. Last night I lay awake for a long time. I have to go to bed at ten, but can never get to sleep before one in the morning, so I lie in the dark, pondering many things. Last night my thoughts ran thiswise: "How strange it is that I am always in a sort of joyful intoxication, though without sufficient cause. Here I am lying in a dark cell upon a mattress hard as stone; the building has its usual churchyard quiet, so that one might as well be already entombed; through the window there falls across the bed a glint of light from the lamp which burns all night in front of the prison. At intervals I can hear faintly in the distance the noise of a passing train or close at hand the dry cough of the prison guard as in his heavy boots, he takes a few slow strides to stretch his limbs. The gride of the gravel beneath his feet has so hopeless a sound that all the weariness and futility of existence seems to be radiated thereby into the damp and gloomy night. I lie here alone and in silence, enveloped in the manifold black wrappings of darkness, tedium, unfreedom, and winter – and yet my heart beats with an immeasurable and incomprehensible inner joy, just as if I were moving in the brilliant sunshine across a flowery mead. And in the darkness I smile at life, as if I were the possessor of a charm which would enable me to transform all that is evil and tragical into serenity and happiness. But when I search my mind for the cause of this joy, I find there is no cause, and can only laugh at myself." – I believe that the key to the riddle is simply life itself, this deep darkness of night is soft and beautiful as velvet, if only one looks at it in the right way. The gride of the damp gravel beneath the slow and heavy tread of the prison guard is likewise a lovely little song of life – for one who has ears to hear.

Rosa Luxemborg, *Letter to Sophie Liebknecht*

JM

24

The danger of limited love

At university I studied the humanities, but humanity itself I learnt on a crowded train. I recognized the Yugoslav station when it suddenly flashed on my TV screen, though just after the Second World War, it wasn't much of a station – only two huts. One housed a machine gun, and the other, with two doors, the conveniences. We foreigners couldn't read the Slav inscriptions, so the men galloped through one door, and the women through the other, and we all collided at one unisex hole.

The train was equally makeshift but alive. Bodies swung from racks, strangers took turns on each other's knees, and peeped between your legs. There were Serbs, Croats, Bosnians and Slovenes, though you had to be one to know which was which. A former Nazi youth was making his way to Moscow and two Albanians toasted the British Communist leader Harry Pollitt, as our little red flower.

A sobbing girl had lost her luggage, and the other passengers out of their nothing contributed a tattered scarf and a slice of grilled goat.

As our train hiccoughed across Yugoslavia, we exchanged pointed Eastern European proverbs and stories. I bridled when one genial gent informed us that Galicians and Bessarabians would both sell you their grandmother, but only the Galicians would deliver. My grandpa came from Galicia.

"OK, tell us your story," he says soothingly.

"An antisemite," I say meaningfully, "tells a Jew on a train, 'In the town we just passed, you can't find a pig or a Jew.' 'What a pity,' says the Jew, 'we didn't get off there together.' " An old peasant woman suddenly laments that no one has enough pig any more and we all laugh. The German lad exclaims joyously how wonderful it is, for only forty months before we were all killing each other, Serbs, Croats, British, Germans and Jews – which is tactless but true. In the silence that follows, I ponder our tribalism, which is what nationalism really is, and what a blasphemous business it is. The religious greats warned against it.

Paul said, "In Christ there is neither Jew nor Greek" and the Hebrew prophets "Hath not one father created us?" And the last words of a Hindu soldier, as he was pierced by a British bayonet were, "And you too are divine."

I left the train near the Serbo–Croat border. They fondled and kissed me and we swore bratstvo – eternal brotherhood. Later, back home, I was taught Englishness at university and Jewishness at my seminary. But on that train they taught me to be a human being. It's tragic that the killing started up again there, for they were the salt of the earth. It's such a tempting trap – loving your own more at the price of loving others less. Unfortunately that's what modern nationalism means, and it leads to hell.

LB

Some people find themselves caught between two identities and suffer as a result:

TO BE AN ARAB JEW

To be an Arab Jew.
What is this title?
What does it mean?
Are you Arab? Are you Jewish?
Where are you standing?
How can it even be?
You are either Arab,
Or you are Jewish –
Because there is the Arab-Jewish conflict.
But I am an Arab Jew,

The danger of limited love

Because Farha Abdallah
Came from Iraq
Which is Arab country.
Of course when she came to Jerusalem,
She became Farha Mizrahhi.
She is Jewish.
She has been to the synagogue
Every Friday night and Saturday morning.
She keeps kosher.
Her language is Arabic.
The music she listens to is in Arabic.
And her connection to the big world
Is through the Arabic department
Of the Israeli television.
Since she lives in Jerusalem,
She could also enjoy some more
Programmes from the TV station in Amman.
I didn't grow up speaking Arabic.
And through my childhood,
I wasn't able to communicate with my grandmother.
My parents wanted me to speak Hebrew.
Then I went to school and learned English and French.
Arabic has never been a priority for them.
In the housing project we lived in,
People from Persia, Kurdistan, Morocco,
Iraq, Egypt, Bukhara, Yemen
Lived one next to the other
And instead of multi-culture
We heard the national radio play
European and "Israeli" music.
And then there was the Arabic department.
But you don't really listen to it
Because in the projects everybody could hear
What you listen to – and you are
Ashamed to be caught
Being an Arab Jew.

Nava Mizrahhi, *The Tribe of Dina: A Jewish Women's Antholog*

But others manage to transform their experience into a way of building bridges between the two parts of their identity, interpreting one side to the other, thus transforming their pain into something of value to the world.

One such unexpected person was the late Sammy Davis Jr who was about as complicated as a "one-eyed Negro Jew" could possibly be. But in his memoirs he talks about his struggle with racial discrimination throughout his life and some of the lessons he learned.

I memorized certain things, one in particular, "The difference between love and hate is understanding." I kept thinking about it and I realized that it was something I'd found out in the Army, something I'd seen a dozen times since then, but I just hadn't known the words for it. Can you know what a hunk of truth like that does for a guy like me? If I can keep that in mind it's like a bulletproof vest. I know for a fact that when I meet someone who doesn't like me, who hates my guts, that if I sit with him for a while my chances of changing his mind are pretty good. I've just got to give him an opportunity to see what he didn't know or think about before. I realize that there are certain people who are never going to like me, not on toast or on rye. If two World Wars did not wipe out blind hatred then I know I'm not about to. Nor do I really care that much about trying with certain guys. If I look at it calmly, it's an equalizer that some guys need – they're getting kicked around and they've got to let it out on somebody so they find someone *they* can kick around. Okay, but when the guy calls you the name, normally you don't smile and think, "Relax, Charley, it's his crutch." All you know is he just hit you over the head and you want to hit him back, and whether you do or not, it's exhausting. But now, let him hit me with his crutch, I'm wearing a steel hat. If I find somebody hating me because he doesn't want to understand me, then I'm not going to hate him, because I *will* understand him. I'm not going to let him insult me and then exhaust me too.

Sammy Davis Jr in *Yes I Can: The Story of Sammy Davis Jr*

JM

25

When tragedy strikes

Listening to the sounds and images of war in the media, I notice that God's name came up a lot, and I sat back wondering what's in a name, even a holy one. What does it do for us in crises?

A vet told me a name is really a call sign. Pets, for example, don't know their name means them, only that they're wanted. And a philosopher said a name separates you out of the rest of reality. So God can't have a name at all since He is all reality – totality, infinity, the lot.

Yet Moses asked God to tell him His name, and got the answer "I am that I am". You're puzzled! So was Moses. The only person who ever pronounced it was the High Priest, once a year alone, in the Holy of Holies, and after that was destroyed, no one even knew how.

But in crises, personal or political, I don't think the names we ascribe to God help us much, because we don't use them for purification, but misuse them for propaganda, camouflage, personal advantage and as tactical weapons. So they become devalued, and get their meaning confused.

If we want to locate God, I suggest, in place of the question Moses asked, the slightly different question that Thomas Aquinas asked as a child. He didn't say, "Mummy, who is God?" but "Mummy, what is God?" which was very very bright of him. That's the question you encounter in the depths, whenever you're really shaken, whether by war or private tragedy.

One summer for example, four of us had gone on a boating holiday, all good friends. But you never know what your friends are like till you live with them. Who used so much shower water, we couldn't wash up? Who was captain, who was crew? Who shared his plonk but kept his chateau bottles in his bunk?

Then one afternoon that private tragedy struck, which nearly wrecked our lives as well as our holiday. One of us went overboard, and if another one of us hadn't saved him and himself, two people might have perished.

In the shock that followed, these words formed in my mind. "I am the unseen Power, always at work, bringing order out of chaos, good out of evil, new life from destruction."

That was certainly the way it worked in us. We rediscovered each other, the tragedy made our holiday, and I don't think the good feeling it created will ever go.

Neither will those words that formed in my mind. I've recalled them often since in hospitals and hospices, while watching seemingly senseless suffering.

And when I watch the bombs and missiles fall on TV, I suddenly remember how I used to pick unexpected flowers that grew among the ruins during the blitz, and I put my trust again in that silent Power, that like a midwife struggles to bring a new world to birth, from human folly and the pangs of death and war.

LB

26

When religion isn't a help but a hindrance

I feel depressed and low and someone very rightly says, "Oh, Rabbi Blue, I'm so sorry, why don't you cheer yourself up with one of your own jolly Jewish jokes?"

I'll let you into a secret. Most Jewish jokes are so oy-oy-oy and mis, they give me nightmares.

Before the war, I was frightened stiff by the German Jewish ones. Two Jews face a firing squad. One asks for a last cigarette before they fire. "Be quiet," hisses the other, "or you'll get us into real trouble." See what I mean?

After them, came the sad Stalinist ones. A guard catches an old Jew learning Hebrew in a Soviet train. "Are you planning to emigrate?" he asks suspiciously.

"I'm preparing for heaven," says the old Jew quickly.

"But say you go to hell?" laughs the guard.

"Russian, I know enough," sighs the old man.

But I can't tell you the latest crop. Their humour is too black, and many too bitter against religion. What can you expect, when Jews, Christians, and Muslims are having a shoot-out in the Middle East, in cowboy Western style, and "Catholic", "Orthodox" and "Protestant" slug it out in the traditional trouble centres of Europe? Can you blame unbelievers who want no part in the mess?

It's a puzzle why pious people produce such dreadful results. I think it's because the power we worship is so immense, we can't cope and have to make it cosy in our minds. But in making it cosy, we make it partial, partisan and human just like ourselves.

We don't mean any harm. We want to house God in a suitably holy place, make others pious to please Him, and defend Him from His enemies. But He is beyond such partisan love. He needs no home, except in our hearts, and what use is forced piety, for religion was never meant for robots. It is folly to think the Creator of the Cosmos needs our protection against mere human beings.

Indeed, unless our religions help us to be impartial in our love and locate Him above all in our opponents, the result will be a pious punch-up. God will survive of course and so will His goodness, but what about the religions which claim to represent Him?

If you're a paid-up, card-carrying member of one of them like me, have a think about it! And what about a jolly gentile joke to cheer a Jew up for a change? What about "What did the animist say to the Bishop?" or something like that. You know what I mean.

LB

27

Why the Garden of Eden goes wrong

A side effect of some tablets I take is bad dreams, and each night I endure my own private horror show. I wake up with relief, turn on the radio and tune in to a farming programme which soothes me with its cows and compost. I can almost smell the mulch through my transistor. Then there's the familiar voices of the announcers and presenters, and gradually the horror turns into happiness, and I look forward to my nosebag of oats.

But one morning, it was the reverse. For once I had a happy dream, about a girl called Gladys, though I know no Gladys and I woke up reluctantly. The horror was provided by the radio.

In a European election, I heard antisemitism had resurfaced. I felt sick. Six million ghosts marched through my mind – the orphans from the ghetto on the way to the gas chambers and old folk crammed into cattle trucks. Someone said the people there were having a hard time, and they couldn't handle their feelings, so they passed the buck to any minority which couldn't hit back. Was it the start of the same murder scenario as the thirties? I simmered with anger as I went down to breakfast.

My non-Jewish hosts greeted me warmly. They'd prepared porridge specially for me. Had they put salt in it? Yes they had. Well, I didn't want it.

Their faces fell. They'd also bought me a newspaper. I pushed it aside. They exchanged hurt glances. Suddenly I pulled myself up. I also couldn't handle my feelings, making them pay for problems they weren't responsible for. I quickly explained and apologized, before I wrecked our holiday. "Don't worry," they said kindly. "Passing the buck is as old as the hills. It goes back to the Garden of Eden, when the man blamed the woman and the woman blamed the snake."

You must feel the same helpless anger as me as you watch the box and see ordinary people slaughtered and their homes, like yours and mine, the work of a lifetime, blown to bits. Now I've no special political insight. I can only suggest these rules of spiritual hygiene.

Don't make devils out of people you disagree with.

Remember God isn't partial.

Try not to hate your enemy in your heart, even if you fight him.

And if you can't handle your frustration and rage, hand them on to God who alone can purify them. Don't give hell to those around you, whether they're friends, foes, or even your poor old pooch Fido.

An odd thought has just occurred to me. Where was the Garden of Eden where the man blamed the woman, and the woman blamed the snake?

Genesis describes its geography in detail. Some think it's probably modern Iraq, which is truly double-blessed, the most fertile land in the Middle East, lying on a lake of oil. But once again human ambitions and refusal to take responsibility turn heaven into hell.

LB

Lionel has raised the spectre of antisemitism and racism which are difficult topics to deal with – because of their reality and destructiveness, and the way the victim can even become further victimized for attempting to draw people's attention to the problem. There is a famous (infamous?) saying that "just because you're paranoid, it doesn't mean they aren't out to get you", and Jews have lived under such threats from Biblical times. Perhaps the nastiest curses in the Bible are the descriptions of what exile will be like:

And as for those of you that are left, I will send faintness into their hearts in the lands of their enemies; the sound of a driven leaf shall put them to flight, and they shall flee as one flees from the sword, and they shall fall when none pursues. They shall stumble over one another, as if to escape a sword, though none pursues; and you shall have no power to stand before your enemies (*Leviticus 26:36–37*).

Or again in Deuteronomy:

In the morning you shall say, "If only it were evening!" and at evening you shall say, "If only it were morning!" because of the dread which your heart shall fear, and the sights which your eyes shall see (*Deuteronomy 28:67*).

That can be the experience of any minority in any society living in fear of its life – of any refugee, or anyone who does not conform when troubles come to a society. The rabbis record a story that exactly describes the "Catch 22" experience of people trapped in such a situation – a story that is nearly two thousand years old and straight out of today's newspapers.

A Jew passed before the Emperor Hadrian and greeted him.
Hadrian said to him: "What are you?"
He replied: "A Jew."
Hadrian said: "Shall a Jew pass before Hadrian and greet him? Go and cut off his head!"
Another Jew passed and saw what had happened to the first so he did not greet Hadrian.
Hadrian said to him: "What are you?"
He replied: "A Jew."
Hadrian said: "Shall a Jew pass before Hadrian and not greet him? Go and cut off his head!"
His councillors said to him: "We do not understand why you have done what you have done. For he who greeted you is to be killed and he who did not greet you is to be killed."
Hadrian replied: "And do you want to tell me how to deal with my enemies?" (*Lamentations Rabbah 3:41*)

So how does one respond in such situations? With whatever powers of resistance one can draw on – from spiritual searching to armed struggle – because such inhumanity seems to be the problem that every generation has to cope with, whether as victims or oppressors. We have the record of some extraordinary responses to oppression and martyrdom. Someone who emerges from the darkness of the *Shoah*, the Holocaust, is a Dutch woman, Etty Hillesum. Born in 1914, she kept a diary from the 9th of March 1941 till October 1943, when she was taken from the transit camp at Westerbork to her death in Auschwitz. It is a remarkable record of her conscious attempt to dedicate her life to the needs of others under the harrowing circumstances of the Nazi occupation and the destruction of the Jewish community.

I shall always be able to stand on my own two feet even when they are planted on the hardest soil of the harshest reality. And my acceptance is not indifference or helplessness. I feel deep moral indignation at a regime that treats human beings in such a way. But events have become too overwhelming and too demonic to be stemmed with personal resentment and bitterness. These responses strike me as being utterly childish and unequal to the fateful course of events. People often get worked up when I say it doesn't really matter whether I go or somebody else does, the main thing is that so many thousands have to go. It is not as if I want to fall into the arms of destruction with a resigned smile – far from it. I am only bowing to the inevitable and even as I do so I am sustained by the certain knowledge that ultimately they cannot rob us of anything that matters. But I don't think I would feel happy if I were exempted from what so many others have to suffer. They keep telling me that someone like me has a duty to go into hiding, because I have so many things to do in life, so much to give. But I know that whatever I may have to give to others, I can give it no matter where I am, here in the circle of my friends or over there, in a concentration camp. And it is sheer arrogance to think oneself too good to share the fate of the masses.

An Interrupted Life: The Diaries of Etty Hillesum 1941–1943

Why the Garden of Eden goes wrong

Facing the inevitable with dignity was the fate of a couple of American Jews, Julius and Ethel Rosenberg, the first civilians to be convicted as spies and executed in the United States. Much controversy still surrounds the verdict and even more the punishment. The following is their final letter to their children.

Dearest Sweethearts, my most precious children,

Only this morning it looked like we might be together again after all. Now that this cannot be, I want so much for you to know all that I have come to know. Unfortunately I may write only a few simple words; the rest of your own lives must teach you, even as mine taught me.

At first, of course, you will grieve bitterly for us, but you will not grieve alone. That is our consolation, and it must eventually be yours.

Eventually, too, you must come to believe that life is worth the living. Be comforted that even now, with the end of ours slowly approaching, that we know this with a conviction that defeats the executioner.

Your lives must teach you, too, that good cannot really flourish in the midst of evil; that freedom and all the things that go to make up a truly satisfying and worthwhile life, must sometimes be purchased very dearly. Be comforted, then, that we were serene and understood with the deepest kind of understanding, that civilization had not yet progressed to the point where life did not have to be lost for the sake of life; and that we were comforted in the knowledge that others would carry on after us.

We wish we might have had the tremendous joy and gratification of living our lives with you. Your daddy who is with me in the last momentous hours, sends his heart and all the love that is in it for his dearest boys. Always remember that we were innocent and could not wrong our conscience.

We press you close and kiss you with all our strength.
Lovingly,

Daddy and Mommy
Julie   Ethel

P.S. To Manny: The Ten Commandments religious medal and chain – and my wedding ring – I wish you to present to our children as a token of our undying love.

The Rosenbergs.

The Rosenberg Case: We are all your Children, Vicki Gabriner

JM

28

Prescriptions for anxiety

Have a good look at my face on the cover, if your book has one. It's not a beautiful object, just a roundish face with low cheekbones, and a snub nose – a typical East European Jewish face, which you can find two a penny in North West London. Now it's not a Semitic face at all, which is a thin long face with high cheekbones, like desert nomads. And this is no surprise because my ancestors weren't Semites at all. They were the usual goulash of Germans, Celts, Cossacks and Tartars, with an occasional ravishing Viking or Roman. I doubt whether .0001 of Abraham's blood flows in my veins or my ancestors'. Like most other Jews, I am the descendant of converts.

There are other myths too – that Jews always stick together. They don't. Where there are two Jews you get three opinions, and the various parts of the Jewish religion barely speak to each other unless there's an emergency, but these alas have never been lacking.

What are Jews like? Well they don't mug, but they do gamble. They give more per head to charity than any other community, but they like you to know it, on the basis that if you've got it, show it. There's lots of love in Jewish families, but it's a bit manipulative. They used to have a low divorce rate, but no longer, and they're not selfish but self-absorbed, and there's better food than booze at Jewish weddings.

If I'd been given the choice of being something else – blond, heroic and humourless maybe – with high cheekbones, well, I don't know. But I wasn't and I'm quite content.

I'm telling you all this, because I'm getting a little more

racist mail than usual, and also, and I don't believe it's a coincidence, a lot more mail about people's worries.

People feel threatened by recessions, and mortgage payments; have they got AIDS, and do they dare take a test? what will happen to the holiday they booked in Yugoslavia? will the NHS be enough or can they afford private insurance? where will their children go to school?

It's tough when the economic cake crumbles and everyone competes for the crumbs. That's when we want to find someone to blame, to be our devil. But the devil isn't outside us, he's inside us, as I've already said. He's the bit of us which won't take responsibility, which wants to pass the buck, which wants to say everyone is wrong or second-rate except me.

Now there are more honest ways of dealing with worries than that. I've always been a bit anxiety-ridden myself and I pass on these tips which helped me.

Make a list of all the things you've ever worried about and make a tick beside every one that's happened. I find that it's only things I don't worry about that happen, not the things I do – which is quite worrying but in a different sort of way.

Another tip – remember all the people who are much worse off than you.

Now some people, including me, quite rightly turn to God in trouble. But remember religion isn't magic. The cosmos won't go off course to suit your convenience. Nor will your body stay young for ever however much you pray for it. What religion will give you is courage. So if you've got the guts, gaze into your problem, because you won't just see trouble, but God waiting to meet you on the other side of it.

LB

III

Being Your Own
Worst Enemy

29

"Cruel to be kind"

I once witnessed a curious incident at a party. As the other guests got happier, one pretty girl grew paler. Fortunately a friend noticed and restored her with a little wine saying, "This'll cheer you up." And she perked up and laughed.

Then suddenly another chap grabbed her glass and threatened to throttle the first chap. "You're a fine friend," he said.

Our host said nothing but later told me the girl was an alcoholic. The second chap was a better friend to her than the first, for a true friend doesn't buy an hour of ease at the cost of someone's ruin.

It was the same when I was trying to give up cigarettes on doctor's orders. My worst enemies were my friends who weren't prepared to risk a row by giving me hard advice that hurt.

But it's no use blaming others. I've also avoided saying the hard bit, though it was the only thing worth saying.

I knew a couple I was marrying didn't mean the same thing by their promises. But I didn't want to be a spoilsport and a messy divorce resulted. I also didn't admit to a dying girl that she was dying, though I think she knew it and wanted me to help her handle it. But I'd promised her family not to.

On a bigger scale I also said too little too late about the Palestinian refugees, before one side had been locked into its own fear, and the other into hatred. I hesitated for good friends said it would hurt my career.

In the long run, of course, you cease to be credible to yourself or others, if you suppress the truth.

This is stern stuff but this tale illustrates the moral

pleasantly and kindly. I heard it at an alcoholic meeting.

To celebrate their anniversary, a young couple book two rooms at their old honeymoon hotel – one for themselves and another for their young son. But the hotel is over-booked, and they have to make do with only one. They put the little boy to bed and go down to dinner. When they get back, the boy is fast asleep and so in the darkness the couple quietly kiss, embrace and celebrate their marriage.

Next morning as they pack, they find the last page of a letter their little boy has written to a school friend. "And these, my dear Carruthers," it ends "are the very same people who dare to tell me not to pick my nose."

LB

There are no simple answers to the issue of truth-telling, especially when it enters the political arena. The complexity is shown in this piece by Louis I. Rabinowitz, who was the Chief Rabbi of South Africa until 1961. It was part of a High Holyday sermon and his own personal confession of what he saw as a failure in an impossible situation.

Some months ago I received a letter from the State Information Office (of South Africa) to the effect that they wished to ascertain the views of the various churches on the racial question, and inviting me to state the views of Judaism. Let me frankly say that to this day I still feel the bad taste in my mouth when I recollect my reaction to that request. Rarely, if ever, during the quarter century of my ministry has that acute conflict between principle and expediency, between truth and "tact", raised itself in more acute form in my mind. On the one hand every instinct that was within me, every teaching of Judaism, every influence of the ethics of the faith which I profess and teach, the voice of the prophets of old, spoke to me in clear and unmistakable voice. Tell the truth. Lift up thy voice as the Shofar and tell them what Judaism and what God say. Tell them that from the second chapter of the Bible "This is the book of the generations of man" (*Genesis 5:1*), with its rabbinic comment (*Genesis Rabbah 24:8*).

"Cruel to be kind"

"This is one of the fundamental principles of the Torah, since it teaches 'This is the Book of the Generations of Man'", not of Afrikaner or of Jew, not of black or of white, but of man . . . Judaism has utterly rejected the doctrine of racial discrimination . . . Judaism does not know any division of mankind which gives an inherent superiority to a man or a race because of the colour of his skin, but only because of the colour of his soul . . .

That is what I wanted to say, that is what I should have said, because that is what the authentic voice of Judaism says. But could I say it? . . . How could I make a statement on racialism which would constitute a flaunting, decisive rejection of the policy not only of the Government, but of the whole of White South Africa. How could I involve the Community in the possible consequences? And so, having become older and more cowardly, and having developed a modicum of that quality that those who possess it call tact and diplomacy and those who lack it hypocrisy and insincerity, I chose expediency in place of principle. First I hedged as long as possible, until it was impossible to hedge any longer. And then I drew up a statement, always with an eye not so much to the word of God as to the possible repercussions on the Community and having completed it I submitted it for approval, not to the supreme religious authority of Judaism, but to the lay heads of the Community.

Of course I salved my conscience by making reference to the rejection of the racial doctrine by Judaism, albeit cautiously and almost apologetically, but I hedged it about with so many "buts" and "on the other hand", as to take the keen edge off the "sword of words", and when it was approved I sent it off, and duly received a cordial letter of thanks . . .

For the first time I really understood the truth of the statement of the Talmud which on the face of it appears to be a wide exaggeration, "He who dwells outside Palestine is like one who worships idolatry" (*Ketubot 110b*).

Louis I. Rabinowitz, *Light and Salvation* 1965

I suppose our freedom to speak out is in inverse proportion to the responsibility we have to others – that is part of the price of leadership. Some see it differently – perhaps our greatest responsibility is not to our "own" community but to the community in greatest need. Thank God there are always people prepared to take the risk, at whatever the cost, to show the rest of us the right decision. They are the prophets of our time – and all too often the martyrs. The challenge is well expressed by the sociologist Zygmunt Bauman.

> Evil can do its dirty work, hoping that most people most of the time will refrain from doing rash, reckless things – and resisting evil is rash and reckless. Evil needs neither enthusiastic followers nor an applauding audience – the instinct of self-preservation will do, encouraged by the comforting thought that it is not my turn yet, thank God: by lying low, I can still escape . . .
> Evil is not all-powerful. It can be resisted. The testimony of the few who did resist shatters the authority of the logic of self-preservation. It shows it for what it is in the end – *a choice*. One wonders how many people must defy that logic for evil to be incapacitated. Is there a magic threshold of defiance beyond which the technology of evil grinds to a halt?
>
> Zygmunt Bauman, *Modernity and the Holocaust*

JM

30

Suffering from love

I knew a lady who sat by the phone waiting for a call that would never come. "She was better off without him," I commented, "and one day she wouldn't even remember his name. She just couldn't let him go, but until she did, no one would replace him in her life."

This is what happened with her. She went for advice to a friend who promptly fixed her up with a blind date. Now it takes courage to go on a blind date, or apply to a dating agency, or answer a personal advert, especially if you're a woman, and it takes even more courage to tell your friends about it. But that's what she did, and this is the advice she got. She was surprised it was so extensive.

A divorced man told her, "Meet the chap in a café, never in your home or his."

A woman friend added, "Don't feel you've got to give him your telephone number, dear. If they can't wait they're not worth waiting for – that's what I say."

"If you go to a singles club, you'll bump into your ex," warned one friend knowledgeably.

"Even romance requires discrimination," added another. "Some dating agencies are clergy-approved. Some are commercial but caring and some are quite dicey."

Now this advice may seem more practical than pious, so here's the religious bit and it's the most realistic advice of all. It doesn't come from a textbook but from experience, my own.

For many dreary years, nobody fell in love with me, and I wondered if I looked like something from outer space, though I'd all the normal limbs and bits. The truth was, I wasn't ready for love. I didn't even know what it meant. My dates suspected it and ran a mile.

When I caught religion, I was told God loved me as I was, without conditions. This mind-blowing fact helped me to like myself, and this helped me to like other people, not as I wanted them to be, but as they were. I tried really hard to see them as God saw them. Something had to unlock in my soul, before human love could happen.

Now if you're suffering from love – or the lack of it – you may have to ask yourself some painful questions. Is the stumbling-block a social one outside you, or a spiritual one inside you? Are you ready for real love and is that what you really want? Sex can sometimes be part of the package, but it needn't be, so don't get excited now. Just curb your exuberance and wait for it.

It was only when I began to feel for others, not just use them in the second-feature movies that chase through my mind or manipulate them as part of a private numbers game, that I noticed one of those others liked me as I was. And for the first time I actually recognized it!

LB

There's a little poem that echoes Lionel's thoughts and even his style. By a rabbi called Norman Lipson, it was a delightful surprise to find it in what is normally a rather solemn journal.

> Singles gather together
>   Like religious Jews on Yom Kippur,
> Fervently praying for contact
>   With the "other".

> "May my make-up not run,
>   Don't let me act the fool.
> Let my conversation be witty,
>   May my breath be fresh

Suffering from love

And my deodorant last.
Help us, O Lord, make contact
With the 'other'."

True prayers and hopes
Are not uttered in Temple;
They're offered at crises
In parties and bars.

Norman Lipson, *Journal of Reform Judaism*

Somewhere between fantasies of love and the "real thing"
that we have to work on is a universeful of expectations,
flirtations, romances, disappointments and temporary
arrangements. It is a universe filled by the songs of the great
popular composers – and though many of them just feed on
the fantasy, others contain enough experience and truth to
help. At least we know that someone else came this way
before us and lived to tell the tale.

Someone who could turn out a dazzlingly witty song to
fit any occasion was Lorenz Hart, the first partner of
Richard Rodgers. He seems to have been a complex man –
witty, brilliant, incredibly generous, fun to be with, but at
five foot nothing tall, with a feeling of self-disgust about his
appearance, homosexual at a time when it was even more
difficult to acknowledge than today, and with a drinking
problem that ultimately killed him, he was also a lonely,
tragic figure. So when he writes about being alone, without
love, we can believe him.

Spring is here!
Why doesn't my heart go dancing?
Spring is here!
Why isn't the waltz entrancing?
No desire,
No ambition leads me.
Maybe it's because
Nobody needs me.

Spring is here!
Why doesn't the breeze delight me?
Stars appear!
Why doesn't the night invite me?
Maybe it's because
Nobody loves me.
Spring is here, I hear!

Dorothy Hart, *Thou Swell, Thou Witty: The Life and Lyrics of Lorenz Hart*

A different sort of a person was the lyricist Howard Dietz. According to his biographers he was a man of great charm and wit, who had to struggle in his later years with Parkinson's Disease. One of his songs, written with his major collaborator Arthur Schwartz, seems to fit the theme of the struggle with loneliness. There's a scene at the beginning of the Hollywood version of their musical, *The Bandwagon*, with Fred Astaire, playing a dancer down on his luck, and seemingly a has-been. Arriving alone at the station in New York, he strolls the length of the platform, singing to himself the haunting "I'll go my way by myself".

I'll go my way by myself,
Like walking under a cloud.
I'll go my way by myself,
All alone in a crowd.
I'll try to apply myself
And teach my heart how to sing.
I'll go my way by myself,
Like a bird on the wing.
I'll face the unknown.
I'll build a world of my own.
No one knows better than I myself
I'm by myself
Alone.

JM

31
"When love congeals . . ."

As the divorce statistics suggest, falling in love is just the beginning of something, not the end. The rabbis, who were very serious about marriage, were also pretty realistic about it, as the following story suggests.

A Roman matron asked Rabbi Jose ben Chalafta: "How many days did it take God to create the world?"

"Six days," he replied.

"And what has He been doing ever since?"

"Making marriages."

"And is that all He does?" asked the woman. "I could do as much myself! I have men slaves and women slaves. In one hour I could marry them all."

"Though it may appear easy in your eyes," said the rabbi, "yet every marriage means as much to God as the splitting of the Red Sea."

What did the woman do when Rabbi Jose was gone? She took a thousand men slaves and a thousand women slaves, placed them in two rows, and said: "Let this one take that one, let this one take that one" – and in a single night she married them all. The next morning the women came to the house of their mistress. One had a cracked skull, another a bruised eye, a third a broken arm. "What happened?" she asked.

And each one replied: "I will not live with this one – I will not live with that one . . ."

Then the woman sent for Rabbi Jose, and said to him: "There is no God like your God, and your Torah is beautiful and praiseworthy, for you were in the right."

And he replied: "Did I not say that though a good marriage may seem an easy thing in your eyes, to God it means as much work as the miracle of the splitting of the Red Sea?" (*Genesis Rabbah 68:4*)

Part of the problem in marriage is that our expectations are too great and the reality too tough. As Erich Fromm put it: "To love somebody is not just a strong feeling – it is a decision, it is a judgment, it is a promise."

Some of our false expectations come from the popular songs that surround us – and even if they are a lot tougher today, they still express the same hopes, and needs, as this one by Ira Gershwin.

> There's a somebody I'm longing to see:
>   I hope that he
>   Turns out to be
> Someone who'll watch over me.

> I'm a little lamb who's lost in the wood;
>   I know I could
>   Always be good
> To one who'll watch over me.

> Although he may not be the man some
> Girls think of as handsome,
>   To my heart he'll carry the key.

> Won't you tell him, please, to put on some speed,
>   Follow my lead?
>   Oh how I need
> Someone to watch over me.

> > Ira Gershwin, *Lyrics on Several Occasions*

But Gershwin could make his own ironic comment on the problems caused by this type of song.

A treatise on popular song lyrics by semanticist S. I. Hayakawa in the quarterly *ETC* (Winter 1955) has a good word for the realistic approach of songs in the "blues repertory": e.g., Eddie Green's "A Good Man Is Hard to Find". But he deeply deplores the emotional effect on listeners of such songs as "The Man I Love", the Rodgers-Hart "My Heart Stood Still" and "Blue Room", the Whiting-Donaldson "My Blue Heaven", the Johnny Black "Paper Doll", and many others. The "literary slop" in these songs and their like saddens Mr H. because they doom us to what speech-pathologist Wendell Johnson has named "the IFD disease": I for "Idealization (the making of impossible and ideal demands upon life)"; F for "Frustration (as a result of the demands not being met), which in turn leads to Demoralization." The final step? D – Demoralization or "Disorganization" – leads "into a symbolic world ..." and "the psychiatric profession classifies this retreat as schizophrenia ..."

An excerpt quoted from the first-mentioned corruptive lyric: "Every night I dream a little dream, And of course Prince Charming is the theme ..." One is warned that this sort of romantic whimwham builds up "an enormous amount of unrealistic idealization – the creation in one's mind, as the object of love's search, a dream girl (or dream boy) the fleshly counterpart of which never existed on earth". Sooner or later, unhappily, the girl chances on a Mr Right who, in turn, is certain she is Miss Inevitable; and, both being under the influence of "My Heart Stood Still" (which even advocates love at first sight), they are quickly in each other's arms, taxiing to City Hall for a marriage licence. On the way he sings "Blue Room" to her – she "My Blue Heaven" to him. But, alas, this enchanted twosome is wholly unaware of the costs of rent, furniture, food, dentist, doctor, diaper service, and other necessities. There is no indication in the vocalizing "that having found the dream girl or dream man, one's problems are just beginning. Rather ... *all* problems are solved". It naturally follows that soon the marriage won't work out, when "disenchantment, frustration" and "self-pity" set in. Shortly after, they buy paper dolls, not for each other, but ones they can call their own. This comfort is, however, temporary. Subsequently, he, helpless, is in the gutters of Skid Row; she, hopeless, in a mental institution.

This is the case history of just one couple, but typical. There are millions more through whose ears infiltrate the airings of Broadway's demoniac love potions. Thus, with the continuous dinning of so-called sentimental song strength-sapping us, eventually we must become an enfeebled nation, paralyzed by IFD. Q.E.D.

Ira Gershwin, *Lyrics on Several Occasions*

Lorenz Hart tried to correct the oversentimentalized view of love in his own way – though the result, if a bit sado-masochistic, is no less romantic.

You don't know that I felt good
When we up and parted.
You don't know how I knocked on wood,
Gladly broken-hearted.
Worrying is through.
I sleep all night,
Appetite and health restored.
You don't know how much I'm bored.

The sleepless nights,
The daily fights,
The quick toboggan when you reach the heights –
I miss the kisses and I miss the bites.
I wish I were in love again!
The broken dates,
The endless waits,
The lovely loving and the hateful hates,
The conversation with the flying plates –
I wish I were in love again!
No more pain,
No more strain,
Now I'm sane, but . . .
I would rather be gaga!

"When love congeals"

The pulled-out fur of cat and cur,
The fine mismating of a him and her –
I've learned my lesson, but I
Wish I were in love again.

The furtive sigh,
The blackened eye,
The words "I'll love you till the day I die".
The self-deception that believes the lie –
I wish I were in love again.
When love congeals
It soon reveals
The faint aroma of performing seals,
The double-crossing of a pair of heels.
I wish I were in love again!
No more care.
No despair.
I'm all there now,
But I'd rather be punch-drunk!
Believe me, sir,
I much prefer,
The classic battle of a him and her.
I don't like quiet and I
Wish I were in love again!

Lorenz Hart

The psychoanalyst Abraham Barzeli spells out the central problem at the heart of our relationships – that sharing a life with someone opens certain possibilities and closes off others.

> To relate is to sacrifice, and though no one would deny their need to relate, we all do deny our need to sacrifice . . . but it lays there under the surface no matter what our attitude to it is. Our reluctance to look under the surface, and the endless social phenomenon of marriage and divorce, seem to be rooted in the

desire to return to the Garden, where no sacrifice was required. Well, we were expelled from the Garden and it was destroyed. We now live in the world that God filled with suffering, and our striving for wholeness is tied to the world and the people in it.

Abraham Barzeli, "Reflections on the Myth of Marriage"

JM

32

A doubter's advice on spirituality

A curious incident ended an interfaith conference I attended many decades ago. We old-timers were congratulating each other, when a young man, whose name and religion none of us knew, startled us out of our wits. "Now as we believe the same thing," he said sternly, "we must confront all doubters immediately with the choice between belief or . . ." and he drew his hand expressively and chillingly across his throat.

Was he serious or was he taking the mickey? Some giggled nervously. Some pleaded pressing engagements. Amused, yet half alarmed for my friends, doubters all, I tackled him sharply. "Religious people have no monopoly of goodness," I said. "Even atheists know life isn't just things." I also handed him a book I was reading – *The Thoughts of Marcus Aurelius*, the ancient Roman emperor – but the young man wasn't interested.

I recommend those same thoughts to you. Now Marcus Aurelius was a soldier who wrote them on active service. Also, he wasn't a believer in the Christian or Jewish sense. So his thoughts are practical, not ecclesiastical.

He doesn't tell you to love your enemies, instead he gives you some tips on how not to hate them. When you get up in the morning, he says, tell yourself: "Today I'll meet a fool, an ingrate and a bully." Then while your mind is still clear, meditate on why they are as they are and you are as you are and the difference between you if any.

I do just that. I meditated on a woman, God rest her soul, who always did me down, but I remembered she was an exile who could never shed her insecurity, so I just gritted my teeth.

Then there's this chap who's a disaster area. He came to dinner and trod on my dog, which bit him. He crashed into the cooker and fused the lights. To fix the fuse, he stood on a chair and promptly went through it. Meditating on him, I realized he just wasn't wired up right. My anger melted and was replaced by a brilliant idea – next time finger food on plastic plates!

Meditating on the world in the morning, before it highjacks your heart, you also realize how many leaders of men are slaves to their unresolved infantile feelings. Stalin was paranoid and Hitler megalomaniac. Some, like Mussolini, try to prove their virility to themselves or to long-dead fathers. So millions die, human and animal. That's the problem of this century – tiptop technology highjacked by primitive feelings.

The advice of Marcus Aurelius turned some of my own angry feelings into pity. And I recommend it, for the violence of war and recession, releases the violence in us.

A lady told me she was a doubter who learnt a lot from religious people. Well, I'm a believer who learns from doubters. As Marcus Aurelius said, "If a God exists, follow Him, and if He doesn't, try to be like Him." That's a bridge between all of us, believers and doubters alike, who acknowledge a spiritual dimension to life, more worthy than our gut feeling and instincts, beyond our passing prejudices and passions.

LB

33
Anger hygiene

A friend of mine looked at war pictures on the box one night and just couldn't stop. The horror was so compelling, sleep was impossible. So she just went on watching, and had a hard time next day in the office.

I know what hit her.

All destruction is addictive. I used to join a queue of people at a building site, provided with a platform and a peephole. The platform was crowded when we watched the old building being demolished, but the queue disappeared when all you could see was the painstaking construction of the new building that replaced it. Destruction is so much more dramatic than construction.

I used to suffer from the same problem as my friend. When I watched the pictures of the Falklands War, I felt the adrenaline flowing in me, and my anger surging up. I couldn't control it, and it was my mother who brought me down with a bang. "For God's sake, Lionel," she said, "simmer down, you're becoming a misery to live with!" She was right!

I remember at that time going off to the library to find a book on philosophy to cool me down. While leafing through one, I suddenly stopped in my tracks. "Don't look too long into the abyss," said Nietzsche, "or the abyss might look into you." In other words, if I looked at horrors too long, I would become a horror myself.

But you can't insulate yourself from the world and to keep away from current affairs would be cowardice – so how do you deal with the violence in you?

Now some people try to get rid of their anger by acting it out. I don't recommend it, it does you no good, and it's not fair on your nearest and dearest, who have to suffer it, when they've got problems of their own.

Some smash cheap plates but I don't recommend that either – in any case plates aren't cheap any longer, even in charity shops.

A long walk with a dog works it out of your system. But what about going into a place of worship and praying your anger out of you? Pure things do not reflect back our anger, they absorb it.

You can also sing or laugh your fierce feelings away. That's how we coped during the blitz. As the sirens go, a husband calls to his wife to come to the shelter. "Sarah, Sarah," he shouted, "come quick, the sirens are sounding."

"Wait a minute," she shouted back frantically, "I've got to find my false teeth."

"But honey," he pleaded, "they're dropping bombs not bagels."

Bagels by the way are Jewish bread rolls, very delicious, where the dough is boiled as well as baked. Jews eat them with cream cheese and smoked salmon offcuts.

But the best way to express surplus feelings isn't comfort eating but to use them for good. Find out if they need some help in your local hospital, or help a charity or organization that sends comforts to refugees of whatever nationality, or make a pile of sandwiches and give them to the homeless and the hungry who haunt the big stations. (Yes, you'll get an occasional rebuff, but you can take it!) Why not walk an old person's dog? By helping them, you help yourself. Where do you find out more? Well, ask at your local church, or start off with the Citizens' Advice Bureau. Off you go now, don't .nope, just get started, and have a good morning.

LB

34
Hidden hurts

My friend Bruno is big and blond, and built like a gorilla. His friend Maxi is even more so. They are gentle giants who play patience, collect old junk, and have decorated their squat so it looks just right for Rembrandt's mum. They share shirts and shorts, and only fall out when they go for the same girl, which is often.

"Bruno, what's happened?" I exclaimed when I saw him last, for he had one leg in plaster, and one eye, formerly blue, was now black.

"It's that Maxi," he said gloomily.

"Why, he's a monster," I replied.

"You're so right, Lionel. All that religion makes you so wise. Why do I waste my time on rugger? You must give me lessons!"

"He needs a psychiatrist, Bruno," I said.

"Three," said Bruno. "Maxi's a big chap. It'll take two to hold him down."

"Well, I'll speak to Maxi," I said. "You'd better not see him again!"

"Not see Maxi?" said Bruno. "That's a bit uncharitable, Lionel – not quite Christian maybe, though don't get me wrong. After all he had a little provocation – though not much, mind," Bruno added fiercely.

"Bruno, what did you do to Maxi?"

"He's in hospital," said Bruno sullenly, "with two busted ribs. I'm taking him out today. It was, as you say in England, a little tiff between two friends!"

When I dropped in on them again, the two big men sat on either side of one slim girl. All three were placidly playing rummy and hitting each other affectionately with crutches.

To celebrate Maxi's return they'd redecorated their squat yet again, which now looked more suitable for Mondrian's mate.

I watched them with bewilderment, envious because I can't express hurt feelings so naturally. I suppress them instead, and pay for it with depression, sulks, grudges and storing up anger for a future Chernobyl. "In religion niceness isn't enough," I thought. "It's too easy. Openness and honesty require more courage."

And I remembered a text from the Bible which supports my gentle giants. "Thou shalt not hate thy brother in thy heart," says the Book of Leviticus, chapter 19. "Thou shalt surely rebuke him," which is just what they'd done.

Now, of course, you're not as big as Bruno and Maxi and you don't have to be as boisterous. And take care when you rebuke your brother, because he may have feelings he wants to express as well.

But the Bible is right, because hidden hurts take even longer to heal than bones. An old nanny I knew said the same thing very simply. "It's better out than India, (in, dear – get it?) but be polite and always say pardon!"

LB

35

Blessing your enemies

After the war, when school ended I used to hitch south. At the Med, I always turned left to Provence, never right to Spain, because that country held bad memories for me, though I'd never been there. Two of my cousins – the heroes of my childhood – had died fighting Fascism in the Civil War.

I'm grateful to package holidays which finally got me across that frontier, because they have abolished the horrors of history. The look-alike hotels have no past, just as their poolside romances have no future. Each wave of new tourists wipes away all traces of the one before.

But on the Costa Blanca, around the anniversary of my cousins' death, someone said there was a civil war memorial in nearby Alicante and reluctantly I had to remember them. When I asked a tourist office how to get there, they tried to fob me off. Wouldn't I prefer a mock medieval banquet with chicken and chips? Yes, of course, but "No, I wouldn't!" So after a lot of telephoning around, they grudgingly gave me a train number and the name of a stop.

In Alicante, I fortified myself at the bright new burger bar, and then found the tram. It clanked past bright tourist bars, then past solid serious banks – then along a long dusty road, lined with old lorries, to a starker Spain, without bright lights, that was tourist-free. When I enquired haltingly, "Guerra Civil?" one old man nodded and led me to the door of a youth hostel where he shook my hand.

Along a corridor behind another door was the saddest prison I'd ever seen, unaltered since the civil war. Each grey cell contained one table, one tin plate, and a straw mattress on a stone floor. They looked onto a gaunt chapel.

I sat by an old woman – the only worshipper – and as she prayed for the fallen heroes, I thought of my cousins and responded, "Amen" – "So may it be!" I followed her into the yard, and bowed my head as she laid red paper flowers by a plaque marking the execution-place. Perhaps my cousins had died here. Then I read the plaque and froze. I had prayed for the wrong martyrs, the ones my cousins had given their lives against. I suddenly remembered with tears how a great-aunt's hair had turned white when she heard the news of their death.

But can you unpray prayers? It seemed both wrong and ridiculous to carry on the Spanish Civil War into the after-life and eternity. Worn down by conflicting feelings, I reluctantly responded "Amen" again. The Spanish Civil War which ended in 1938 had finally died in me. Bless them all, bless them all, I thought wearily, the long, the short, the tall, the lot!

May God bind them all into the gathering of life.

LB

Lionel has caught very precisely the tragic anonymity of so much of human suffering and death. It may take at least a generation before we can admit that *our* victims and *their* victims are *both* victims and equally to be mourned.

The following poem, dated "Lwow 1940", was found among the papers of a Jewish woman, Ewa Wistrich, who survived the war in Poland by pretending to be a Catholic. It is believed to have been written by her.

Amongst all the anguish and troubles,
And a long, intense yearning
There lived in us a world of dreams and marvels,
And a togetherness, real and living.
Sometimes anxieties oppressed us
But in the heart there flickered hopes –
Faith and strength within us
That fate would change the course of life.

Blessing your enemies

That inner peace of spirit
Would return with times once known ...
That we shall see fields ploughed
For a healthy harvest – and in us repentance.
Joy of freedom and new strengths
Will blossom – we will build another future
To heal the wounds which were cut
By distress and human malice!
And laughter will appear again
And a sun-lit countenance,
For nowhere will there be hardship.
And this I wish for us all.

Ewa Wistrich, by permission of Harriet Wistrich

JM

36

Inner violence

Many years ago in Italy, I was crossing the road to a cata-
comb, engrossed in a guidebook, when a hooting car bore
down on me. Not knowing my left from my right, I stood
my ground and gaped, which disconcerted the driver and he
hit a hot-dog stand. In the pandemonium that followed, I
and the driver, whom I'll call Alfredo, became fast friends.

He always meets me at the station, and we're off, racing
round ruins that he and other Alfredos, ancient and
modern, have knocked about a bit. He's a fine driver. It's
just the violence of his feelings behind a wheel which
frightens me.

"Stupid crows!" he yells at some Sisters of the Holy
Ghost, who leap on to the pavement, looking as if they'd
just seen one. A large lady steps into the road to squint at a
belfry. It's a mistake. "Dutch bitch!" growls Alfredo. His
remarks are racist, sexist and antisemitic.

When we stop, he reverts to the pious, unprejudiced, nice
guy he is.

I'm also a nice guy – mostly. But there's plenty of violence in me too.

I couldn't cope with my anger, for example, when I
watched Italy play Argentina in a soccer match on TV. I
was puzzled by the strength of my own passions, because I
couldn't care less who won, and have no interest in soccer –
indeed the only goal I've ever scored was against my own
side. So why was I so partisan, first for one side, then the
other?

I also get angry when two people are talking quietly. I
suspect they're making antisemitic remarks about me,
which they aren't, usually.

Also, like lots of children, I wanted to get rid of my parents – in fantasy, of course. I couldn't allow myself to murder them, so I let them fade away through a painless but final illness, and I could at least go to bed when I liked.

Violence is part of our nature, what being human is about. So don't feel guilty about having it, just responsible about what you do with it.

Firstly recognize it in yourself, not just in someone else. It's often disguised as depression. Then you can deflate it with a joke, or use it to write a murder story, or defuse it by reading one, or you can scream it out at a wrestling match where it's part of the ritual, or like me, you can use an older ritual, and recite at God those violent verses in the Psalms nice prayer books leave out, like "Happy is he who dashes thy little ones against a rock", though that's too strong for my stomach, or, "Let their way be dark and slippery, let the angel of the Lord persecute them, let destruction come upon them unawares."

But it's better than hitting a human being, because God can absorb the violence.

Who knows? He may find it more authentic than the usual soft soap.

But whether you use it, or pray it away, never, never become the dupe of your inner violence and act it out in real life. That's the difference between Alfredo and old Adolph, and between me and a murderer.

LB

As Lionel points out, the Psalms are full of expressions of anger which are directed to God. (Some of them are to be found in the section "Out of the depths", at the end of the book.) And though a lot of it is about betrayal by other people, God comes in for a fair share of criticism in the Bible as well. The whole Book of Job is a challenge to God's justice in the world, and the prophet Jeremiah accuses God of being like a treacherous stream of water that dries up just when you need it.

One of the most unexpected examples of such anger with God occurs in the Book of Ruth. I had tended to dismiss the story as being too sentimental till I began to study it properly. It seemed too cosy – a "pastoral idyll". But I began to understand something of the suffering of Naomi, the other main character in the book, when my mother died. She was survived by her mother, my granny, who was utterly destroyed by her loss – her little girl had died. It did not matter that my mother was fifty years old and had grownup children of her own. Granny's own special little child had died and she followed her not long after to the grave.

In "Ruth", Naomi, living away from her native land, lost her husband and two sons – the Hebrew text actually calls them her "children", literally the ones she gave birth to. Naomi is left alone except for her two daughters-in-law, and she sends them away even though they try to stay with her.

> Go back, my daughters, why come along with me? Do I have more sons in my womb to be your husbands? Go back, my daughters, go! I am too old to be with a man. If I said I still have hope, and spent this very night with a man and even gave birth to sons, would you wait till they had grown up, would you shut yourself away from being with other men? No, my daughters! I am more bitter even than you, for the hand of the Lord has gone out against me (*Ruth 1:11–13*).

Naomi is emptied out, of family, security, of a future and of hope. Silently she walks back to Israel, accompanied by Ruth. But when she reaches Bethlehem, her bitterness bursts out in the form of a poem:

> Don't call me Naomi (pleasantness),
>   call me Mara (bitter)
> for the Almighty has marred me.
>   I went out full
>   but the Lord brought me back empty.

Inner violence

Why do you call me Naomi
    when the Lord has spoken against me
    and the Almighty has harmed me!

Naomi shouts out her anger against God – but God does not
seem to mind. No thunderbolt strikes her. In fact this marks
a turning point in her journey back to life. There is a God she
can shout at, even in the emptiness. She is not really alone. In
fact, now she can see for the first time that Ruth is with her.
In Bethlehem, at the start of the harvest season, she begins to
look for a new husband for her daughter-in-law. Life goes
on.

JM

37

Streetwise

In 1936 the economic depression lifted and both my parents found work. They left home before seven in the morning and came back, worn out but grateful, after eight, to get me my supper and put me to bed. We no longer had to hide from the rent man.

They paid the grocer, for my tea, and told me to pass the time till they came home, at the play centre or Hebrew classes. I did neither. I discovered the street instead.

As the gasman lit the street lamps, I watched other children through curtain chinks, sitting round their tea tables with their families. I must have felt lonely and resentful, because I remember tying a crying boy to a lamppost. He mustn't go home either. He must stay and play with me. I discovered I could be a bully.

I became streetwise quickly. I learnt to get into the cinema without paying – slipping past the usherette, changing seats constantly and escaping through the skylight in the gents. I could also wheedle chocolate out of strange grown-ups, by putting on childish charm.

At first, I thought the street was empty, but then I bumped into other children, who also wouldn't or couldn't go home and roamed the streets like me. They coalesced into gangs who fought like modern nation-states. I was allowed into one on probation because of my age and inexperience. But being not quite seven and small had its advantages. It was easier to steal for the gang at Woolworths, while the bigger boys and girls created a diversion.

It all ended in tears. One day my parents came home early to give me a treat. But I wasn't there. I was roving the London docks with my gang.

There was a colossal row, so serious I couldn't compre-hend it. Some of the gang were taken into care, and some were sent to Borstal. I wasn't a juvenile delinquent, just an infantile one, so I escaped and ended up in religion, not in a reformatory.

Even nice people harbour a criminal inside them. Some call him the evil inclination and some original sin. I remem-ber a charming lady at a party. "I would murder or steal to help my family get on," she said. Everybody laughed but I felt uncomfortable. Was it a figure of speech or did she mean it?

When you see gangsters and criminals at the cinema or on TV, it's like looking at animals in the zoo. They're inside the cage and you're outside it. You don't belong to the same species.

But don't fool yourself – you do! Never take respect-ability for granted but thank God on your knees for it every day because only an accident or knife-edge separates you from them. I learnt that lesson before I was seven. If you haven't learnt it yet, you could do a lot of damage and be very dangerous, so take care!

LB

If Lionel had not triumphed over that childhood experience of street life, he might have put the blame for his fate on his parents. But what about the pain of parents forced to leave their children for long periods of time for the sake of earning a living? This is the theme of countless Yiddish songs. Often it is about a mother singing a tearful lullaby: "Sleep, my child . . . your father's in America trying to make money to bring us over to him". But sometimes the father himself speaks, as in this song by Morris Rosenfeld. Born in 1862, he grew up in Warsaw, learned tailoring in London and moved to the US, where he barely earned a living in the sweatshops and nearly went blind. But he became the poet of the workers, his songs about their lives being sung at mass rallies, and spreading throughout Europe. Nevertheless he died in 1923, poor, alone and embittered.

MEIN YINGELE — MY LITTLE SON

I have a little boy,
a fine little son,
when I see him, it seems to me
I own the whole world.
But I seldom see him,
my little son, when he is awake.
I always meet him when he sleeps.
I only see him at night.
My work drives me out early
and makes me come home late.
Strange to me is my own flesh and blood.
Strange to me the look of my child.
When I come home shattered,
wrapped up in darkness,
then my pale wife tells me
how nicely our child plays,
how sweetly he chatters, how cleverly he asks:
"O Mother, good Mother,
when will he bring me a penny
my good, good father?"
I listen and yes, it must,
yes, yes, it must happen!
Father love blazes up in me.
My child, I must see him.
I must stand by his cot
and see and hear and look.
A dream stirs his lips:
"O where is Daddy?"
I kiss the little blue eyes.
They open, O child!
they see me
and quickly they close.

There stands your father, dearest,
there you have a penny!
A dream stirs his lips:
"O where is Daddy?"
I become sad and oppressed,
bitterly I think,
when you finally wake, my child,
you won't find me anymore.

From *Jiddische Lieder*, Hai and Topsy Frankl

How many parents face that same tragic experience around the world? And how many wake up one day to realize that they have created that experience for themselves when it was not really necessary, because they put different priorities first – and making a better living became more important than living?

Getting it right as a parent is hard enough at the best of times. Mothers seem to get the brunt of the complaints – as Wendy Greengross puts it: "A mother's place is in the wrong!" But fathers can acknowledge their own failures too – and with a bit of courage on both sides there are chances to make up, as in this poem by Saul Gottlieb.

I cannot recall precisely what was on my mind
at breakfast, when I turned to you and shouted,
insisting that you act as you should act
(rather as I thought you ought to act,
you being twelve now and approaching manhood),
when I in rage tore the jar from your hand
and ruined your food with the sugary stuff,
and you in your young manhood rose,
bewildered love and hatred sounding,
clashing, wordless in your throat,
and ran out into cold of morning
without your jacket on.

How to Get Up When Life Gets You Down

Whatever it was you compensated,
when you had gone I recalled my grandmother,
once when I was about your age,
enraged because we never said 'good morning'
when Danny and I would meet her, mornings,
and I with that stupendous insolence
for which I was famous then,
told her to go to hell,
and she cried, "Respect!"
and I sneered, "Respect?
What does it mean, Grandma, dear?"
Hurt and silent, she hobbled away.

Now I have tasted such bitter fruit
of seeds so carelessly scattered.
O Michael dear, there are demands
that cannot be required, cannot be returned,
until we both know the meaning of the word.

Whatever it was, a lost dream or a failure,
you knew it was myself I scolded,
for when you soon returned
we touched each other
as Mother and I do after quarrels,
each finding the fault in himself.

Saul Gottlieb, Commentary Magazine, 1955

JM

38
Loss of Status

She had silky brown hair, and long lashes framed her liquid brown eyes. These she half closed as she gazed at me with a sideways glance. The convent buildings slept in the heat haze behind the trees. We were alone. As I came closer she suddenly pressed herself against me. We lay side by side in the grass, and I fed her cow parsley. Occasionally she butted me in the belly to express her feelings.

It was Emily, the convent goat, who had taken a shine to me, and when they came to lead her back to her pen, she again half turned to give me one last lingering look.

To be the recipient of love is a wonderful thing, and that night I lay awake fantasizing. She could bed down in my garden shed. I would feed her cow parsley and she would feed me her yoghurt and reduce my milk bills – an arrangement both reasonable and Franciscan.

Next morning before breakfast, I rushed to her meadow and halted in shock. She had changed into a very nasty goat, unlike the loving animal of yesterday. She stood on a hillock braying boastfully, and butting the other nannies. She gazed at me briefly, bared her teeth and brayed again in triumph.

At breakfast the nice nun who attended to the goats and the guests saw I was hurt. "Don't judge her harshly," she said, "that goat has suffered." Her sad story turned my anger into pity. Emily was a brown goat in a herd of white ones, who never accepted her. And having no kids, she had lost all status in her herd, which obsessed her.

Cleverly, under the guise of love, she had manipulated my attention, because the attention of any human being gave her the status she craved and schemed for. Now having got it, she had no more use for me. Like many modern people, she rejected the real things of life for their shadow. I said farewell to the kind nun and returned home. My letter box was so jammed with junk mail, I could scarcely open the door. A coloured credit card would make me the envy of other borrowers. An exclusive travel ticket would entitle me to use a lounge and loo only sat on by better-class bottoms. A club announced it was exclusive to executives.

"Enjoy the goodies but beware the poison bait!" I said to myself. Enjoy the good opinions of others, but don't let your self-respect depend on them. Remember poor Emily who sacrificed true love for status, the substance of things for their shadow. It's a pity she couldn't chew her way out of the garden into the chapel, to meditate on the time when God will sort out His sheep from the goats. For, when all we creatures pass before Him, He will gaze into our substance, not at our status in the herd. Such knowledge now would serve us well in the life of the world to come – and it would give us better balance in this world too.

Now you may know the stories of "A man called Horse" and "A fish called Wanda". Well, here's the sad story of "A goat called Emily". Ponder it well!

LB

39

Making a mess of your life

My friend Fred is fascinated by the enormous prices paid at art auctions and asks me to take him to the latest art exhibition to see what all the fuss is about, which I do. We get there and find we're the first viewers. They haven't even finished unpacking the exhibits. Fred, who was a brickie once, conscientiously stacks the debris into neat piles, until a banshee wail from an attendant freezes our blood. The debris are the exhibits and Fred has tidied the art out of them. We are escorted away in disgrace, Fred bewildered and protesting.

"That's art?" he says incredulously.

"Yes."

"That's the stuff they bid millions for?"

Fred is not the only confused connoisseur. A wealthy lady goes to an art gallery to add to her collection. "That's perfect!" she says in rapture to the dealer, "a panel of virginal white, with stark blackness growing out of its centre – a classical yet erotic statement at the same time. I'll buy it."

"Certainly if you buy the building with it, madam," says the dealer. "It's the light switch."

But producing art is even more confusing. I know, because I was thrown out of the art class as a kid – I was so bad. While the others drew conscientious daffodils, I could only produce smudges, thumb prints, and trickles of watercolour that meandered hopelessly over the paper.

Many years later, I said enviously to another friend Irene, who was a real artist, I wish I could paint too. "Why don't you?" she said. So I laughed and showed her one of my normal disasters. She gazed at it intently and then said

"Now let's improve it!" And she dribbled turpentine over it, tipping the canvas this way and that to make a gorgeous mucky mess. "Now lets turn it upside down," she said to my astonishment "and gaze into it again. What does it look like to you?"

"A fire in a grate," I answered, beginning to get the hang of it.

"And what do you see in the flames?"

"A face in a tree," I said. She passed me a brush.

"Make me see that face too!" Well that became the first painting I ever exhibited.

If you can't paint, but want to, I recommend her method. Don't be scared of making a mess. You may have to ponder many messy paintings before the right one is born. There's no short cut. The same advice applies to writing. You have to study many false starts before you know what you really want to write. They're not false at all, they're necessary.

And it also applies to life. If you've made a mess of your life, and who hasn't, don't waste your energy kicking yourself or pretending it never happened. Your mess is important, if you have the courage not to disown it.

The messes we make in life are the best teachers God has given us, provided we respect them and don't sweep them under the carpet. It's only through them that we learn compassion and kindess and what it feels like to be an underdog or one of life's losers. You don't find out such things by success, you know. And these are very important lessons indeed. True, they might make this life more complicated for you, but you can't get into eternal life without them.

So study the mess you've made like a book. Gaze into it like a painting. You won't see only the painful past but also pointers to a better future. You might make out the face of God in your mess, gazing back into you with love and understanding. I did! That's how I discovered Him.

LB

40

"For those who are hissed on stage"

JULJAN TUWIM

I discovered I could write songs, or at least put funny words to familiar ones, in my youth group cabaret days. At medical school I even found some rudimentary tunes of my own and for a couple of years would haunt the folk clubs of London, screwing up my courage now and then to perform in the interval as a "floor singer". On one occasion, at Bungies, I shared the interval with a young American who also wrote his own songs. I told him I liked his songs, and he told me, that like myself, he had also written a song about someone who had committed suicide. He probably won't remember the incident, but it is nice to say I once shared the billing with Paul Simon.

But standing up in front of an unknown public has its hazards. I once visited a new club. That very afternoon I'd written a new song, something sentimental about nurses, and I was desperately eager to try it out, unaccompanied voice, before an audience. And halfway into the first verse, the words began slipping away, and then the tune, and I ground to an embarrassed halt, face burning, wishing to high heaven that the stage would open up and swallow me – anything to get out of that awful situation. I slunk off stage, convinced I would never show myself in public again. I suppose I was already very shy, and "performing", always an ordeal, was a way of pushing myself into some sort of public recognition. But this awful incident set me back a long way. For years afterwards, I just had to think of those moments and my cheeks went bright red, my heart thumped loudly and I was an adolescent again as embarrassed and ashamed as on that awful night.

I cannot remember when I "got back on the horse again".

Probably not for some years, and only after I'd learnt a few guitar chords to strum behind my songs – perhaps holding the guitar gave me a bit of security and protection.

In retrospect it was a "learning experience", and as Heinrich Heine pointed out, "someone who has never made a fool of himself, has never become wise". But it gave me an enormous respect for all performers who daily put themselves at risk before the public, exposing themselves to ridicule or the awesome, burning silence of the embarrassed audience.

That is why I particularly like the following anecdote by Lilli Palmer from her autobiography *Change Lobsters and Dance*. The pain and suffering of learning the craft of acting is very well described and the feeling that almost anything can be borne during that long painful process of becoming an artist if one has the respect and support of a good teacher and the determination to break through.

Within a very short time, I had to admit that Beate had been right, "No craft. No understanding. No taste." Under protest, sometimes in tears, I had to accept it, losing every bit of my film star "poise" in the process. But Elsa taught in the only way you can teach anybody anything: by taking away but at the same time giving something in exchange. She never said, "What on earth are you doing?" without immediately showing me how it ought to be done.

Up to then my acting rules had been simple. I was sincere. If it was a sad scene, I cried. (Easy.) If it was a gay one, I laughed. (Not so easy. Laughter on command is not easy.) It wasn't until I met Elsa that I learned to my amazement that a comic scene must be played dead seriously and that a smile on your face can make a sad scene even sadder.

It was a fight with no holds barred. After our long sessions, I would jump into my car and drive home exhausted and cursing loudly. I cursed Elsa and I cursed myself, in equal parts. But gradually, after several months of nightly drudgery – I couldn't start working with her until I'd finished at the studio – I felt I was

"For those who are hissed on stage"

beginning to understand what she was getting at . . .

Shortly before the war, she left England to work in Hollywood
. . . All that was left of her was a piece of paper she had pinned to
my dressing table with a drawing-pin on my first opening night. I
was to read it through slowly every evening before the first scene.
On it she had listed my ten principal shortcomings, all the things
she wanted me to bear in mind and guard against:

1. Remember you have no charm.
2. Don't *act* adjectives. No need to illustrate what you're
   saying.
3. Iron out those abrupt, hasty gestures.
4. Take your time. Then no one will be bored.
5. Don't mumble.
6. Listen to your fellow actors. That will make *you* interesting.
7. Stay dry. Sentimentality is Mortal Sin Number One.
8. Don't stand with your feet apart. Keep them together.
   You're not in the gym.
9. Stay vital. Monotony is Mortal Sin Number Two.
10. Courage – above all courage.

I kept that sheet of paper for years. Long after I stopped working
with Elsa, I still carried it around with me, pinning it up on every
new dressing table until it was in shreds. In the end, all you
could still make out was the beginning:

1. Remember you have no charm.

Lilli Palmer, *Change Lobsters and Dance*

The clergy are public performers and I suppose that we are
just as susceptible to making fools of ourselves as anyone else.
In the old days you were pretty certain of an audience – but
not any more. And there are many subtle traps for those who
lead others in prayer. The clue to the problem is well told by
that other great "monologist" George Burns. When his wife,
Gracie Allen, retired, he decided to continue as a single act –

though very uncertain if he could succeed without his zany partner.

When I walked out onstage for the first time, Gracie was sitting at a table directly in front of me. I introduced her and the audience gave her the usual standing ovation. Then I did my act. I thought it was pretty well received, even though Gracie got more applause just for showing up than I got for doing my entire act.

Afterward I asked her what she thought of the show. She didn't hesitate. "Wasn't Bobby Darin wonderful?" she said.

Bobby Darin was wonderful, I loved Bobby Darin, but that wasn't what I meant. "Come on Googie," I said, "You know what I mean."

"Well, Nat," she said, "I think you're reciting your monologue. You know how you always say that honesty is the most important thing onstage, and if you can fake that you can do anything? I don't think you're faking it very well. And if you don't believe what you're saying, how do you expect the audience to?"

George Burns, *Gracie: A Love Story*

I heard an equivalent story about a senior rabbi who had a beautiful voice and would chant the prayers regularly in his synagogue. Then one week he stopped abruptly and never did it again. A friend asked him why, and he answered, "I suddenly found myself listening to my voice." So whether one is being true to an audience or true to God the problem is essentially the same, which is why the rabbis insist that "our prayers should be new every day".

JM

41

The poverty of the rich

The little street I used to live in is no longer there. They'd built a block of flats over it, for the little houses it replaced had no indoor loos, and harboured bugs, and my uncle, a six-footer, slept with his feet dangling out of the window. But for the people who lived in those houses, the little street was their club, their community, their world, and they donkeystoned their doorsteps daily. On sunny days they sat on the pavement passing titbits, and in winter they gossiped from bedroom windows.

A crazed woman came to live on the street, who scrubbed her pavement as well as her doorstep and wept whenever horses fouled the road. The children taunted her but Granny said she'd seen too many horrors in Russia, and told me to give her some fish with Mrs Goldstein's compliments to strengthen her brains. When I hesitated, Granny said, "A big boy of six like you frightened of a poor sick woman – well I never!"

I thought of the crazed woman when, in a London club, quite out of my class, I met a man who also knew her. Together we used to play knocking-down-ginger on her door knocker. He was successful and generous with it, inviting me to visit his lovely home, which I did some months later when I happened to be nearby. The houses were beautiful as he said, surrounded by shaved lawns without flowerbeds. I called but he was away and the house-keeper politely refused to let me meet his mother, which was reasonable as I would now scarcely recognize her.

Finding my way out of the estate proved unexpectedly difficult. The streets had no names and the roads no pave-ments. I asked a child if there was a bus, but her nanny snatched her away and told her never to speak to scruffy strangers without a Merc or BMW. There was no village store, only a swift silent bank. Flowerbeds, I learnt, impeded security systems.

Some months later, I bumped into my old friend again and complimented him on his lovely home. "Do you like living there?"

"Of course," he said, "it's the best."

"But do you enjoy it?"

"It's the best," he repeated puzzled. "Everyone should live like that."

Queuing at a bus stop in the rain, I decided I for one didn't. Between the poverty of the little street and the new prosperity, fear had crept in uninvited, poisoning human contact, whose presence no budget could exorcise. I suddenly felt sorry for the rich, who hopefully are only one step ahead of us in the march of progress, humanity's advance guard into the prosperity we all consider our right. How hard to reach heaven and not enjoy it – as frustrating, I thought, as threading a camel through the eye of a needle.

LB

When I was studying in Jerusalem my landlady was an old-time pioneer in Israel who had helped establish one of the first kibbutzim. She was a tough old lady who took no nonsense from anyone. She told me once that she had met some visitors to the country who had pointed to children playing in the street and said how poor they looked. "What do you mean?" she asked indignantly. "They've got homes, they're fed and clothed! You want to see real poverty, come with me!" She marched them off to Rehavia, one of the wealthier districts of Jerusalem. "You see that house over there," she said. "The owner is jealous because his neighbour just bought a new car and his is now a year behind! That's poverty for you!"

The poverty of the rich

The Yiddish humorist Shalom Aleichem took this idea one step further.

A man must always be considerate of the feelings of his neighbours ... So, for instance, if I went out to the fair ... and did well, sold everything at a good profit, and returned with pocketsful of money, my heart bursting with joy, I never failed to tell my neighbours that I had lost every kopeck and was a ruined man. Thus I was happy, and my neighbours were happy. But if, on the contrary, I had really been cleaned out at the fair and brought home with me a bitter heart and a bellyful of green gall, I made sure to tell my neighbours that never since God made fairs had there been a better one. You get my point? For thus I was miserable and my neighbours were miserable with me.

Shalom Aleichem

JM

IV
That's Life

42

How to live with what we lose

In some ways, life is all about coping with loss – from the first time the breast is withdrawn from our hungry mouths to our last farewells. The rabbis suggested that when we are born our hands are clenched as if we wish to grasp the entire world, and when we die they are open, as we give everything up. That life is a constant giving up is so obvious that we know it in different ways at all times – but it is so unacceptable in the rush and energy of life that it catches us unawares every time. Long before I knew much about life or love I could write in the chorus of a song:

> For life is also learning
> How to live with what we lose
> Love that may confuse
> And linger on.

There are lost loves and lost lives on our journey, and sometimes reading about the pain of others or the way they coped can help us accept our own.

Here is Bob Dylan toughing it out:

> Strike another match, go start anew
> And it's all over now, Baby Blue.
> Bob Dylan, *Bob Dylan: Writings and Drawings*

But Lorenz Hart could write for someone older who's loved and lost too many times:

LITTLE GIRL BLUE

> Sit there
> And count your fingers.
> What can you do?
> Old girl, you're through.

> Sit there
> And count your little fingers.
> Unlucky little girl blue.
> Sit there
> And count the raindrops
> Falling on you.
> It's time you knew
> All you can count on
> Is the raindrops
> That fall on little girl blue.
> No use, old girl,
> You may as well surrender.
> Your hope is getting slender.
> Why won't somebody send a tender
> Blue Boy, to cheer
> Little girl blue?
>
> Dorothy Hart, *The Life and Lyrics of Lorenz Hart*

To lose a lover may be sad or bitter, but there is always the hope of finding them again, or at least of finding someone new. But the death of one we love is of a different order. The Bible records King David's reaction when his child died.

> Then David got up from the earth, washed and anointed himself and changed his clothes. He went into the house of the Lord and worshipped. Then we went to his own house and when he asked they set food before him and he ate. Then his servants said to him: "What is this thing that you have done? You fasted and wept for the child while it was alive, but when the child died, you got up and ate food."
>
> He replied: "While the child was still alive, I fasted and wept; for I said, 'Who knows whether the Lord will be gracious to me so that the child may live?' But now he is dead; why should I fast? Can I bring him back again? I shall go to him, but he will not return to me." Then David comforted his wife Bathsheba (*2 Samuel 12:15–24*).

Here the writer Pamela Melnikoff reflects on the death of her father.

How to live with what we lose

Even if love
Were in truth the force men say it is,
Do you think then that there would be no death,
No severance, and no more suffering?

For though love
Can in its singular way work miracles,
Weave sonnets out of household words, raise marvellous
    tombs,
Turn labourers into kings and shuffling crones to queens,
And make a child to the last fingernail,
It cannot halt the fissure of a cell.
Love can bring light where only darkness was,
And yet not keep the darkness from the door.

So all that love,
The brave boy, shining and omnipotent,
Worshipped by gods, obeyed by emperors,
Immortalized in verse and stone and sound,
Giver of life, can finally achieve
When all is ceded, is to make more sad
That last relentless parting of the ways.

                Pamela Melnikoff, *Jewish Chronicle*, 7th May 1982

Before the loss itself is the "losing" and the sometimes
unbearable pain of watching someone we love wasting away
and dying before our eyes. Whether it is with dignity or
desperation, our sense of helplessness can be overwhelming
for we cannot know what comfort if any we really bring.
Sometimes the dying do more to reassure the living than the
other way round. I had the privilege of visiting an old friend
in Jerusalem in the weeks before her death from cancer. I
found myself writing the following poem – partly in reaction
to the shock of seeing the physical changes in her, partly in
wonder at the inner strength and warmth she conveyed. Even
at the time I noticed how far I reverted to the clinical detach-
ment of my medical training, left behind for twenty years, as
a way of daring to look at her. But it also freed me to accept

the reality of what was happening and meet the real inner
person who was still there. Reading it from time to time
brings her back.

> She is grey
> grey
> death is leeching the colour
> from her face.
> Note the swollen ankles
> the concealing head-scarf
> the matchstick frame
> so frail.
>
> She is still there within
> warm
> precise
> tender.
>
> The sketches are too pretty.
> That is not her beauty.
> Capture instead the friends around her
> whose turn it is to give
> and share
> and hold
> and wait it out.
>
> Capture the calm
> the laughter
> the softness of memories
> the ebb and flow of pain
> the life still about her
> and within her
>
> not that grey, grey face.
> Not yet.
> Not ever.
>
> For Sarah Kamin, Jerusalem, 13th August 1989

How to live with what we lose

Writing like this may help bring someone back to us, though sometimes it even works the other way round. I once knew a very gifted young Israeli girl. From a secular background she found herself suddenly caught and fascinated by religious faith. I was in regular correspondence with her through the stages of her journey, trying to help her understand the intellectual and emotional changes she was going through. And then quite suddenly came the news that she had been killed in an absurd car accident. Miri was very fond of one of my songs. Singing it evokes her memory – and in an uncanny way reflects the questing and the brevity of her life.

> No obligation to buy.
> No obligation to try.
> But if you still yearn
> it's easy to learn
> to fly.
> > Image when the ripples run.
> > Shadow when there is no sun
> > and it's done.

> Life is a children's game.
> Death is the pretty frame.
> So little time
> and only a rhyme
> to blame.
> > Image . . .

> Souls in the market place
> buy success or grace.
> But things that they sell
> are only the shell
> of a face.
> > Image when the ripples run.
> > Shadow when there is no sun
> > and it's done.

How to Get Up When Life Gets You Down

A last word by the American poet Gabriel Preil who grew up in America, but wrote poetry in Hebrew.

A FUTURE WITHOUT A PERHAPS

I cross out so many names
in my little notebook.
But first they were crossed out
by the Lord of Mercies,
the ambusher who leaps
from his forest of shadows.

I cross out name after name
in my little notebook. Feel I am
accountable, deserving black punishment,
as if I were the first
to do what I have done.

Of course, I am only a bookkeeper
confirming cold facts,
who signs, as it were, an edict
that will also apply to me
in a future without a perhaps.

Gabriel Preil

JM

43
Being second best

For many students now, the real news won't be announced over the radio but through the letter box. "Dear Miss or Mr – " the letter says, "you have been awarded a degree in Higher Babylonian Studies with third-class honours." It's a relief, of course, but can you earn your bread with bits of old Babylon?

At a college bar I listened in to two worried students. "If I get a first, I'll try for the Foreign Office."

"And if you don't?"

"Dad says become a parson," he mumbled defensively.

"Don't be defensive, dear chap," I wanted to tell him. "God can make do with second best – He has to – that's all He got from me in the beginning. If I'd been offered a fellowship, a minister of quite another colour might be writing this advice."

But knowing this has stood me in good stead. People join congregations for the oddest reasons. They may not want to live by their faith, but they certainly want to die in it, and your cemetery is conveniently close to the buses. Some join because of the bridge and some because their boss is a member too. Whenever I want to rise up in righteous indignation, I remember my motives weren't that pure either and I become much nicer.

If your flock get on your nerves, I pass on two bits of advice my rabbi taught me, adaptable to any denomination. Any congregation which doesn't want to get rid of its rabbi aren't real Jews and any rabbi who lets them get away with it, isn't a real rabbi. Also remember if they were saints, you'd be paying them to minister to you and not vice versa.

You can cope quite well with all their shenanigans provided your own faith stays firm. But alas it doesn't; it gets more dicey as the years go by. The texts which seemed so straightforward in college don't stick when you apply them to people you know. And scholars can't decide if Moses is man or myth.

But there's a different type of evidence, inside, not outside you.

To be blunt, you invoked God to make a living. To your relief He came, and for a while you see Him everywhere. He's the beggar by the door, and the treasurer who hands you your pay cheque. He's the AIDS victim, the chairman and the spouse or lover you'd like to do the dirty on.

It's more than you bargained for. You can of course turn your back on Him and He'll go away, because He won't stay where He isn't wanted, but then you'll become bored or bitter as ministers sometimes do. But if you accept Him you'll have to grow like Him. It's tough going but you'll become your own evidence and convert your third-class degree into a first-class blessing.

"See, you've got your First at last. It's a pity no one will ever know it except you. Who says God hasn't got a sense of humour, dear chap?"

LB

44
God's absence

If God is very present in the Bible, the people of Israel and
the individual prophets could also experience God's absence:

> Your words were found and I devoured them,
> and Your words became my joy,
> the delight of my heart,
> for I am called by Your name,
> O Lord, God of all creation.
> I did not sit in the company of scoffers
> and rejoice,
> because Your hand was upon me I sat alone
> for You filled me with indignation.
> So why is my pain eternal,
> my wound incurable,
> refusing to be healed?
> Why are You like a deceitful stream,
> like waters that fail?
>
> JEREMIAH 15:16–18

The Israeli poet Nathan Zach captures in his own way that
emptiness, whether it be the absence of God or just an
absence in one's life:

> Nothing comes.
> The night wind stirs its darkness
> like night wind stirring its darkness.
> Nothing comes.
>
> Nothing comes.
> The door that was closed and opened
> opened and closed.
> Nothing comes.

151

Nothing comes.
Legs crossed, lamp on the table,
a shadow and an undershirt.
The one who entered is the one who left.
Nothing comes.

Nathan Zach, "The Static Element", *Selected Poems*

But is God really absent or are we just unable to see? The Yiddish poet Yankev Glatzhteyn moved from Lublin, Poland to the United States in 1914. He somehow carries over into the new world some of the familiarity with God of the old.

LIKE A MOUSETRAP

Like a little trap,
a shabby synagogue on Long Island.
Only a handful show up for prayer.
No one knows
if even God
drops in there.

The rabbi
is Conservative.
From his synagogue study
he drops God a note,
care of the old address:
Come and hear my sermon about You *shabbes*,
don't forget.

Only a handful show up for prayer,
plenty of room for God's glory.
No one knows if God
will sneak in for an hour.

Selected Poems of Yankev Glatzhteyn

So is God absent or are we just incapable of recognizing God's presence? Glatzhteyn has another suggestion about this.

God's absence

YOU SHOULDN'T BE TAKEN ABACK
(NACHMAN BRATZLAVER TO HIS SCRIBE)

In case you're taken aback, Nathan,
by people nowadays and the way they carry on,
you have to understand – in the soul-workshop upstairs
there's been a brouhaha for some time now –
since they're all out of suitable souls
to refurbish
for new incarnations.

The whole soul-depot is a washout,
everything ripped and picked and fly-specked.

Eh, years ago, souls used to present themselves
spic-and-span, like the newborn.
It was a pleasure – "smooth a few wrinkles
and off you go" – right into a new body.
Now you can't locate a mendable soul anywhere.
It's all vile, musty, and threadbare,
shot through with sin.

Upstairs they sit – patching, piecing rags together,
once splendid creations of good stock
all scratched up now.
Do you realize, Nathan,
what damaged goods
people are made of now?

So – in case you're taken aback
by people and their ways.
What can a mere mortal do
with such secondhand souls?

Selected Poems of Yankev Glatzhteyn

The Nobel Prize winner, Saul Bellow, has recorded in his novels the pain and suffering of today's urban lives, and he too has something to say about souls.

It has only been in the last two centuries that the majority of people in civilized countries have claimed the privilege of being individuals. Formerly they were slave, peasant, labourer, even artisan, but not person. It is clear that this revolution, a triumph for justice in many ways . . . has also introduced new kinds of grief and misery, and so far, on the broadest scale, it has not been altogether a success . . . For a historian, of great interest, but for one aware of the suffering it is appalling. Hearts that get no real wage, souls that find no nourishment. Falsehoods, unlimited. Desire, unlimited. Possibility, unlimited . . . The idea of the uniqueness of the soul. An excellent idea. A true idea. But in these forms? In these poor forms, Dear God! With hair, with clothes, with drugs and cosmetics, with genitalia, with round trips through evil, monstrosity, and orgy, with even God approached through obscenities? How terrified the soul must be in this vehemence.

Saul Bellow, *Mr Sammler's Planet*

Yet Jewish tradition still asserts:
"My God, the soul You have given me is pure."
And it teaches that just as the soul fills the body, so God fills the world, they belong to each other. But what do we do in those dry periods of time when somehow the two seem unable to meet?

JM

45

God is waiting for you in your fears and doubts

You do everything religiously right and God walks out on you. Then you do everything that seems religiously wrong and He walks back in again. That's how it was with me.

I was grateful when they gave me a scholarship to study for the ministry, and I willingly conformed to suburban ways to repay them. I admired them because they were responsible folk, not just respectable, who also gave their time as well as their money to charity.

But one day I had to face facts. As far as I was concerned, God had gone out of the system, and it was no use chasing Him round and round the liturgy.

So feeling fed up, I reverted to my old ways and joined some artists on their way to a rave-up in Copenhagen. Somewhere beyond Bremen our car dissolved into a cloud of rust, and the party began then and there. I wandered round town, and ended up in a decrepit caff by the docks.

And there I saw her! Elegant, chic, pure Paris and utterly out of place. When she agreed to dance, I couldn't believe my luck.

They were giggling their guts out at the other tables and the penny dropped. She wasn't a she, but a he – not a homosexual but a transsexual, a woman in feeling, who'd been born into a man's body. "Don't worry," whispered my friends. "We'll get you out of this, we can hitch to Copenhagen without a car." As I got up to go, the old familiar inner voice returned. "Sit down!" it said. I sat down, surprised and relieved. "Good boy!" said God.

I escorted her to the opera and to tea at smart hotels. Like many of her kind, she didn't want sex, only recognition of what she felt she was. Two years later, I heard she'd taken an overdose. I was grateful God had used me to give her a good time, because for people like her, life was even tougher than now and it had played her a dirty trick.

What did I get out of it? Not sex as I've said, but sparkling conversation, and the envious looks of other men, which was a new experience. I also got back God!

If you've lost Him too, perhaps your religion has become too cosy. Perhaps He's waiting for you outside it – in your fears and theological doubts – in hot issues like women's lib and embarrassing ones like transsexuals, in Palestinian refugees if you're Jewish, and anti-Jewish prejudice if you're not.

Some elderly nuns were put out to grass, for quietness and contemplation. Instead they make meals and wash men's undies for AIDS sufferers. Their refectory has become a gymnasium for exercise and massage. That's how these nuns got back their youth.

If you come to a frontier, and play safe and refuse to cross it, then you can only return to banality and boredom. But if you go forward, and take the risk, and cry "help" when you slip, then that's a real prayer, and that's how you get God back.

LB

46

Suffering endured is the evidence

Conversion's a touchy business in a multi-faith society and an old friend of my mother's got so agitated about it she burst into verse without realizing it. "Hetty, Hetty, watch out, there's missionaries about – don't let them through the door!"

My mother stays calm. If they're clean-shaven she might let them in, if they're shaggy she won't. She never could abide beards, never. Her old friend departs in a huff and Ma says, "Lionel, you're the rabbi, do we let them in or not?"

I ought to agree with her old friend, but temperamentally I'm more of a convertee than a converter. Life's a bewildering puzzle and anyone who can fit another piece is welcome.

Now I've been a disappointment to my converters, and some still pray for me. But my mother prays against them – so what can you do? But I want to reassure them. Though I've never fallen into any font, because of their Christianity, I fell in love with love and met God unexpectedly in committees, discos, and during services. And because of some Hindu missionaries, I think cosmically about creation and my own place in it.

Perhaps in a decade of evangelism, conversion new-style doesn't mean switching to the rival church down the road, just helping each other to goodness, and leaving the rest to God.

Anyway here's some helpful tips to converters about what turns me off and on. Texts taken out of context turn me off and playing happy families makes me suspicious.

But if a converter trusts me with his doubts I'll try to trust his faith. If he doesn't doubt – well we're just not on the same wavelength. Also he's got to listen to me as well as lecture. Perhaps I'll convert him, that's the risk he runs.

Some weeks after this some missionaries do appear on our door step. It's raining cats and dogs, so in they came, theology notwithstanding. "Would you hear our message, ma'am?" they say to Ma.

For some reason Ma replies in a fake Chicago accent. "You put 'em all together and what've you got – tiggledy diggledy doo!" and then totters triumphantly to the teapot.

"Thank you, ma'am," they say bewildered and turn to me. But their theology doesn't impress me either, and they think they've failed, poor wet dears. But I want to reassure them too.

One rainy day, when I'm soaked to the skin and about to bite my friend's head off, I'll remember how polite they were in the same situation, and a bit of me will change and become a bit nicer.

And that's a kind of conversion, isn't it?

Speaking personally, I have never been converted by what people say, because words are too easy, and I can trade texts as well as any. I am touched, changed, converted even, by what people are, because every worshipper imperfectly incarnates whatever God he or she worships. And the outward sign of such incarnation is suffering endured without bitterness or passing the buck.

LB

But what happens when you do convert to another religion? I suppose it depends a bit on the religion, the demands it makes upon you and the people you live with afterwards. Not many convert to Judaism – under two hundred a year in Britain. After all it may take up to five years in the most orthodox circles, though "liberal" groups may take you through the process in about a year – and in Israel it can be even quicker. But what are you at the end of that? Since Jews are a "people" as well as a "religion" it takes a lot of integrating into the "family", and there's sometimes a suspicion of newcomers – who in their right mind would want to experience Jewish suffering? In America they are more open about discussing these problems and have even invented a new term: "Jews by choice", as opposed to "Jews by birth". After all, you don't go through all this business to become a "convert" but to become a "Jew".

The following extract comes from a talk that has been very helpful to people experiencing some of the "post-conversion" problems. Perhaps it applies to all of us who make the difficult journey into the world of another people.

It seems to me that the real work of conversion begins after the formal conversion. Before the conversion one has almost a special status in the community, one comes to learn, to experience the Jewish calendar and Jewish life. After the conversion one is a Jew, but not yet a Jew. Tradition teaches: A convert is like a newborn child. The growing up begins now. One enters a new country with a new language, a different religious language, a new culture, new customs and tastes, a new rhythm of the year with new celebrations, and a new family and community. But this growing into a new life happens alongside the memory and experience of the past life which cannot just be put aside. Entering the Jewish community is more complex than just adopting a new religion. It means becoming part of a new community on many levels.

However, the convert begins with an inevitable basic insecurity. This is experienced as a pressure coming from outside to be more Jewish than a born Jew. In reality the pressure often comes from within. It is necessary to analyse whether such insecurity comes from being a convert or from one's own personal feelings of inadequacy which feed into this new situation.

For example, I found myself being overly concerned with the technicalities of performing all the rituals as meticulously as possible. There is nothing wrong with that but I used to get very upset when I realized that other Jews did not do everything properly! Clearly some of my concern had to do with insecurity. But part of it, and I think that is a more important aspect, had to do with learning. Only by doing the rituals can we learn what they mean to us, not only as an outer experience but as an inner one. Then they can become part of us and become easier.

However at the same time I was also pulled into a search for the pure "essence" of Judaism. This meant going beyond all these rituals and practicalities which seemed at times to be unnecessary. Perhaps this had something to do with my previous religious tradition which had a strong tendency to rid itself of all superfluous trappings. So the main effort in these first years was to find a balance between these two concerns – to feel at home with the ritual life without losing sight of its deeper religious purpose.

Dorothy Magonet, "The Experience of Conversion to Judaism", *European Judaism*

JM

47

"You might as well live"

I found a dog on my doorstep. He stayed contentedly with me for two days, while I found a lady who wanted to give him a home. But just when I found her, the dog bolted and was never seen again. There should have been a happy ending to the story but there wasn't.

That's life – a messy business whichever way you look at it – like running after a moving bus, or knowing how to live just when you're past it and the oldest swinger in town.

Most learn to cope somehow, but if you're a perfectionist, like a girl I visit in Germany, it drives you potty. She regularly makes a date with death in her diary. When the day arrives she postpones it, but occasionally she attempts suicide, and I have to visit her in hospital.

"Have you come to condemn me?" she says defensively.

"No you're just a bit impetuous, old girl. This life's limited and there's an awful lot of eternity, so why rush it?" She looks relieved and bucks up and tells me some friends are forming a group to analyse her despair.

"Can I join?"

"No Lionel, you're too frivolous. But give me a wise Jewish saying."

I oblige with some Dorothy Parker:

> Guns aren't lawful
> nooses give
> gas smells awful
> you might as well live.

"Be serious," she sniffs. "Look at the horrors in the papers and on the radio. Why are you so attached to life?"

"Because I'd bungle my exit," I reply, and to cheer her up, I tell her about a Romanian student I once knew who jumped off a roof and landed on a lady in the balcony below. They lived together, not unhappily, for many years. She sniffs again so I try to be serious and honest. "Because I'm a coward. Because you never know what's round the corner, or if there's a silver lining, or even a golden one, in tomorrow's budget. Because the world's my work and it feels wrong leaving any job unfinished. Because this world's such a fascinating place, I'm addicted to it. It's amazing how people can redeem their unhappiness through art and kindness and comedy! Look," I tell her, "the *Traviata* we saw together was based on TB and the *King Lear* we queued up for on madness. Our world isn't beautiful despite its horrors but often because of them, though I hate admitting it. If our troubles don't break us they're the source of whatever grandeur or depth we've got." My passionate defence of life surprises her. It does me too . . .

But all this death talk reminds me I must make a new will and when I get home I tell my mother. "If I go first you'll be able to lunch at the Ritz."

"Don't be dreadful," says my mother, sincerely upset. But next morning I hear her asking my aunt if she's ever been to the Ritz.

"Atta girl!" I say and toast her in tomato juice – *Le Chaim* to Life!"

LB

This is a disturbing postscript to Lionel's remarks about suicide. Jacobo Timmerman ran a newspaper in Buenos Aires, *La Opinion*, in which he championed human rights and social justice. As a result he received death threats from left- and right-wing death squads alike. In April 1977 he was arrested by an extremist faction of the Argentinian army and was held in captivity and tortured for thirty months. He describes the two temptations that would have meant an escape from his situation – suicide or madness.

Aside from suicide, there's one other temptation – madness. These are the only two temptations, or rather the only two strong emotions I experienced during my thirty months of imprisonment and beatings. Strong emotions because their repressed violence enables them to overpower time. And time is not an easy enemy.

To reflect on suicide does not mean that you're going to commit suicide, or decide that suicide ought to be committed. It means introducing into your daily life something that is on a par with the violence around you. Managing to introduce into that daily life an element on the same level as the violence of that other element. It's like living on an equal footing with one's gaolers, those who beat and martyr you. Sharing with oneself a non-inferior capacity, one equal in magnitude to that of one's oppressor. This self-imposed state of equality functions as a compensatory mechanism. It's with you, has the force to be with you, is created and structured in that place, that prison, and will afterwards be missed or remembered.

More than a decision or a hope, it's an occupation – its dimension so profound, so biological and awesome, that it's a palpable presence. Impossible to confuse with any other sensation, it introduces the possibility of achieving a level of destruction akin to the destruction unremittingly being inflicted upon you.

The word "suicide" is not linked, in the mind of the beaten and tortured prisoner, with any other connotation. Nor to the consequences, possibilities, remorse, or pain that it will produce, or the defeats that the act presumes. It is simply what it is, with its own taste, smell, form, and weight. And it fills the Time of the prisoner's time, and the Space of the prisoner's cell.

He can measure the wall-to-wall distance inside his cell and wonder whether his head will break if he hurls himself against that wall with all his might; or he can imagine the feasibility of puncturing a vein with his nails. All this inherent violence transmits a sensation of physical capacity and inevitability to the prisoner who's undergone torture. It contains an element of romantic audacity, the sense of a completed story.

There's pride in the idea of potential suicide. It's the primary temptation in response to the continual humiliation from one's torturers.

But at some point you must reach a decision to abandon the idea, for it can become too obvious a subterfuge. In fact, it already has become a subterfuge, for you realize that you're not going to commit suicide and once again comes the feeling of defeat. You're humiliated, and the humiliation is justified. Your world is utterly reduced, and the fact that you've told the torturers nothing, and that you've survived, doesn't occur to you. These are not usable values in this world of cockroaches, vomit dried on your clothes, bits of half-raw meat strewn on the ground. A world in which the sphincters must endure their gross intestinal content until you're authorized by a guard to go to the toilet.

Suicide is a usable value because of its definitive, hopeless nature. And can anyone within that obscurity of torture and darkness conceive that the place where he is, the space where he is, is anything other than definitive and irremediable?

Hence, where the possibility of suicide no longer exists, with its splendid image of a raging bull ready to confront the bull-fighter's truth – that suicide which in the darkness of one's cell has the sombre, austere, incorruptible flavour of vengeance – when that possibility of suicide no longer exists, there remains the temptation of madness . . .

I awaited the protective mantle of madness, but it did not come.

I was unable to tame the beautiful bull of suicide, nor did I fling myself on its horns and drench its back with my blood.

I kept going, and here I am.

Jacobo Timmerman, *Prisoner Without A Name, Cell Without a Number*

JM

48
Cemeteries

About 1990 BC, some people believe, Sarah was buried and Abraham marked the spot with a stone. Ever since Jews place little stones or pebbles on the graves of friends and family to record their visits.

At the Jewish New Year the cemeteries are crowded. On the gates are written "This is the house of life" and ice cream stalls nearby do a lively trade. Inside Abraham's spiritual descendants are pretty lively too, wandering around graves, singing out "Amens" and greetings.

An old lady points at me. "That's Harry Bluestein's son, you know – Harry the Tailor. His son's in the papers now. Harry would have been proud of him." I wonder. "Do you remember," she rambles on, "how Harry brought sick cats and dogs back home, and put flea powder on them when your ma had the neighbours in for tea?" I do.

The row rocked the street for weeks. He was like that with all strays, human and animal. I transfer a pebble from a nearby grave to my father's.

I wander away and notice a stone with a stark inscription – just a name and two dates – born in Berlin, died in London. I remember her – a stiff Prussian woman, who followed her Jewish husband into exile. He died, they had no children, and she sat stiff and solitary in an alien synagogue.

She did her duty – not everyone did.

I bribe a boy with a cornet to find me another pebble – no two, I tell him – pebbles, not cornets, because there's another German woman I want to remember. Sally Goldstein, aged twenty-three, who gave her life for Kaiser and country as a stretcher-bearer in the First World War. That's all I know about her. I noticed her name on the wall of a ruined Berlin synagogue and it stuck in my mind, because it was my mother's maiden name. Another thought strikes me too. My father also fought in the First World War – on the other side of course. Perhaps he shot her, but that's an awful thought for another day. She gets her pebble. Someone should still remember her sacrifice.

At the cemetery gate, a beggar sings out, "Charity redeems from death". I give him a coin to remember Kittie Wilkinson – a non-Jewish woman I saw in a bolted and barred stained glass cathedral window. During a cholera epidemic in Liverpool, she took in everybody's washing and disinfected it in her own boiler. It's just what Dad would have done, so I run back to his grave, and reconsecrate his pebble to Kitty.

That night in bed, I count pebbles, not sheep, cocooned in memories.

LB

49

The party's not over

In December, I got a letter from the BBC reminding me I was supposed to give a religious talk and time was up. So is my inventiveness. I get an inspiration. Why not practise what I preach and let Him decide?

Well, what did He want? I screwed up my eyes in prayer and promptly registered a load of fluff, only one sentence made even grammatical sense. "The party's not over till the fat lady's stopped singing." I consigned that too to file 13.

Just before Christmas, I did my hospital visits. I sat on the bed of a woman whose life was on the blink. We held hands, because for one weekend long, long ago we'd been lovers. "What's it like being dead, Lionel?"

"We'll never know, dear, because all you can be conscious of is life – either this sort or the eternal sort." And suddenly I added, "The party's not over till the fat lady's stopped singing."

"What's that?" She almost sat up, and I told her how it had come to me.

Later, she told me that sentence had helped her over the hump back into life. I believed it. Eternal life was reflected in the innocence of her face. For the first time ever our relationship felt right.

I continued with the AIDS wards. "You feel so useless," one of the patients told me. "You're too tired to do much." He lay back and I watched a nurse hug her patient, two friends hold hands, and one patient nurse and hold another. The priorities were so right, I blessed myself. Twice in one day I had stumbled against God.

"Useless," I said. "That you're not. You've given God

back to me again and nobody else has done that this year."

"The party's not over till the fat lady's stopped singing," I added.

LB

50
Old-age woes

It may be that old age is no different from any other age – it just depends on how you look at it and live it. Abraham, at seventy, was a childless old man whose life must have seemed to be over and wasted. Then he suddenly got the call to go on a journey to an unknown place and create a new people and religion.

I heard recently about an eighty-seven-year-old woman who teaches physical fitness at a college and a ninety-three-year-old man who has started learning French. When Lily Pincus lost her husband late in life she studied her experience and wrote a book on bereavement. Then she did more research and wrote another one on the experience of ageing. When she knew she was terminally ill, her editor, a bit embarrassed, asked if she might consider writing something on "dying". Lily said "yes", and apologized that it might be a bit short! She saw the proofs shortly before she died.

The Bible spells out the "bad news" in a famous passage in Ecclesiastes.

> Remember your Creator in the days of your youth, before the evil days come, and the years draw near, when you will say, "I have no pleasure in them"; before the sun and the light and the moon and the stars are darkened and the clouds return after the rain; in the day when the keepers of the house tremble, and the strong men are bent, and the grinders cease because they are few, and those that look through the windows are dimmed, and the doors on the street are shut; when the sound of the grinding is low, and one rises up at the voice of a bird, and all the daughters of song are brought low; they are afraid also of what is high, and terrors are in the way; the almond tree blossoms, the grass-

hopper drags itself along and desire fails; because man goes to his eternal home; and the mourners go about the streets; before the silver cord is snapped, or the golden bowl is broken, or the pitcher is broken at the fountain, or the wheel broken at the cistern, and the dust returns to the earth as it was, and the spirit returns to God who gave it (*Ecclesiastes* 12:1–7).

The following passage is also a bit depressing but the life (and death) of the writer was a total contradiction to what he thought old age meant. Janusz Korczak was the pen name of a Polish Jewish writer and educator, Henryk Goldszmit. His children's stories and radio broadcasts made him a household name in pre-war Poland. He dedicated his life to the needs and problems of children and created a model environment for them in the orphanage that he ran. But he becomes a legendary figure because of his endless struggle to keep the orphanage going under the Nazi occupation and the final march he took with his children into the concentration camp and death on the 6th of August 1942.

Reminiscences make a sad, depressing literature.

Artists, scholars, politicians and great leaders of men – all of them start out with ambitious plans, resolute actions, aggressive, bold moves, they climb higher and higher, overcome obstacles, extend the range of their influence and, armed with experience and a large number of friends, they press – with increasing ease and success – stage by stage, toward their objectives. This takes ten years, sometimes twice, three times that long. And then ...

Then comes fatigue: bit by bit, still doggedly moving in the once chosen direction – only now along a more leisurely road, with diminished zeal and with a painful realization that their life is not what they had meant it to be, that it is not enough, and especially difficult to face single-handed – they find that the only thing they had achieved is more greying hair, wrinkles on the once smooth and bold forehead, failing eyesight, slower circulation and tired feet.

What has happened? It is old age.

Old-age woes

Some will resist, try not to give in, to go on as usual, even at a faster pace and more aggressively, for time is short. They deceive themselves, they fight back, rebel and thrash about. Others, in sad resignation, not only give up but even regress. "I can't go on. I won't even try. What for? I can no longer understand the world. Ah, to recover the years gone by, reduced to ashes, the strength squandered in blundering, the wasteful momentum of the old zeal . . ."

New people appear, a new generation, new needs. Now they begin to irritate him, as he irritates them; first there are some misunderstandings, later – lasting lack of understanding. Their gestures, their walk, their eyes, their white teeth and smooth faces, even though their lips are silent . . .

Everything and everyone around you, the entire world, and you yourself, and your stars, keep saying:

"This is it . . . Your sun has set . . . Now it is our turn . . . Your time is over . . . You say we don't know very much . . . We shall not argue with you – you do know more than we do, you're experienced, but you must let us try our own way . . ."

Such is the order of life.

So it is with man and animal, so it seems to be with trees, and who knows, perhaps with stones as well.

Today is their will, their power, their time. Yours – today old age, and the day after tomorrow – decrepitude.

The hands of the clocks move faster and faster.

The stony gaze of the sphinx asks the eternal question: "Who is it that walks on all fours in the morning, briskly on two legs at noon, and on three in the evening?"

It is you – leaning on your cane, gazing into the dying cold rays of the setting sun.   Janusz Korczak, *Ghetto Diary*

But there is another way of looking at old age. E. Y. (Yip) Harburg was the writer of "Somewhere over the rainbow", and somehow he never lost his zest for life and the dream of a better world still to be fought for and won. At the age of eighty he published a collection of poems *At This Point in Rhyme*, which includes the following:

How to Get Up When Life Gets You Down

At forty I lost my illusions,
At fifty I lost my hair,
At sixty my hope and teeth were gone,
And my feet were beyond repair.
At eighty life has clipped my claws,
I'm bent and bowed and cracked;
But I can't give up the ghost because
My follies are intact.

For more of the "good news" over to Lionel.

JM

51

Third-age comfort

A personal letter plopped through my letter box. I just
opened it and glanced at it, puzzled. A friend wrote asking if
there'd be a celebration for the birthday. Whose birthday?
Then the penny dropped – my birthday because in two
weeks' time I'll be sixty-one.
Now sixty-one is a number you can't get excited about.
At sixty I got an oldie's rail card, courtesy of BR. So while
my mother rides the buses free, I can at least ride the rails at
reduced rates. And at sixty-five, the government and God
willing, I'll get a nice solid pension book. But sixty-one is a
non-event, a number you can't even divide by anything.
But time marches on, and only in one direction, alas, as I
was rudely reminded on the Underground when I politely
stood up for a doddery old gent. "Sit down, sir," I said
politely, for I was once a well-brought-up child.
"Sit down yer-something-self, grandpa!" he spat back.
You see, because your world grows old with you, you just
don't notice the change.
But last week on the same line I bumped into some oldies
like me on their way to Gatwick for a senior citizens' romp
in sunny Spain. I eyed them over my newspaper and felt
much cheered. The "girls" were lithe, lissom and blue-
rinsed. Their "boys" sported bouffant beehive hairdoes
over their grizzled good looks, like rising politicians or
fashionable ladies in the fifties. They were obviously going
to have a ball.
Suddenly I thought of my granny. Now she was years
younger than them, or me now, when she died, but I
remember her still as a very, very old woman, swathed in
black shawls, her boots slashed to ease her bunions. And I

173

realized God had given me and many of my generation, the present of a second youth, a third age – whatever you want to call it, it means another stab at life, another chance to get it right.

And this time I might be more successful. Third-agers are released from expectation. What they've done, they've done – the rest is gravy. And they live more in the present than the future. Also they joke about life while first-agers and second-agers agonize over it.

My mother told my aunt this one, looking meaningfully at me. Some old Jewish women were making conversation.

"Oy Veh!" said one.

"Mmm . . ." moaned another.

"Oh God!" wailed the third.

"Help!" cried her friend.

"Well," said the first briskly, "that's enough about the kids, what about some salt beef sandwiches and a cosy cup of lemon tea."

That's the spirit!

There's another thing that separates us third-agers from the first- and second-agers – we lived through a world war, and remember what it was like, listening to the news, because your life depended on it, and trying to tighten your gas mask and nearly suffocating yourself. But the war had two faces because, listening to the news, we were also witnesses willy-nilly to the power of the human spirit. We saw compassion grow in the concentration camps too, and ordinary people find the inner strength to give their lives for others, their last crust of bread. We know quite well the price good people pay, but we also know that evil is by its nature self-destructive, and in the end the good remains. That provides some third-age comfort in troubled times.

LB

52

A happy day

For my birthday I present myself with an awayday from life. I put on scruffy clothes, and in a nearby caff, breakfast on Coco Pops, open a Regency romance and opt out of reality.

"My Lord," Desdemona dimpled at him, "you must honour your debts of honour. We can live on love."

"My sweet," he whispered urgently, his steely hand gripping the yielding satin that cradled her heaving bosom, " 'twas all a jest. My seat, and three chateaux crammed with Watteaus, are yours."

"What ho, my Lord!" she breathed, roguishly, tapping her fan on his granite jaw.

I sigh with satisfaction. As Granny said, "Love is nice but it's nicer with noodles," and boy, has he got a lot of noodles.

A lady on sticks trips over my foot, recognizes me and plonks herself down. She stares at my plate but it's only Coco Pops, thank God! Then she stares at my book. It ought to be graver and grimmer. "It's got a happy ending," she sighs wistfully. "I could do with one." She points to her feet. "The hospital says they'll get worse."

I get her an Eccles cake, while she peeps at the last page. "What'll they be like, when they grow old like us?"

"They can't," I say. "They're programmed for happiness and God programmed us for growth. Growth means change and change brings pain. It's the price you pay."

"Rabbi, in the geriatric wards they weren't growing, they were disintegrating."

So, I tell her about a teacher in a Rudolf Steiner school, forty years before, who told me even though your body and mind crumble, your soul still grows, only we don't see it because souls are see-through. She spent her spare time trying to teach a brain-damaged kid, with a few months to live, to wave a rattle.

"And do you believe that, Rabbi?" Regretfully, I turn away from Desdemona, gloating over the Watteaus in her chateaux. Well, what do I believe?

"I believe we're on a long journey to perfection, wherever that is. On the way, we go through many experiences, many existences perhaps. They all take us forward, if we accept them, though some seem like failure."

This was serious stuff, so to take her mind off her feet, I promised her my book, after I'd read the ending. She smiled in anticipation.

Later on at the travel agent's, I smile too. Being over sixty, I am now entitled to free tea and biscuits at my holiday hotel. This must be true, because the travel agent notes it on a form.

And to cheer all of us up, though not too much, here's my advice. Though happiness isn't the purpose of our life on earth, there's more of it around than you might think – provided you don't get snobby and despise biscuits and books and other small pleasures, or become greedy and clutch.

LB

I don't know if I would have had a better answer for her feet. As a mere youth, heading for fifty, (unbelievable!) the hints of my own mortality are only just beginning to niggle. I might offer her the Hasidic master Nachman of Bratzlav who fought all his life against melancholia and proclaimed: "It is forbidden to be old!" I doubt if she'd have been particularly impressed.

More comfortable and comforting is, of all people, Allen Ginsberg, one of the greatest and most influential American poets of this century, as well as the most controversial, chronicling the despair of the "Beat" generation and recording in graphic detail his own intimate relationships. But even Ginsberg moved from Beatnik to Eastern meditator and Guru to respectable university Academic, so perhaps it is not surprising at all to find him commentating on the compensations of age.

PROPHECY

As I'm no longer young in life
and there seem to me not
so many pleasures to look forward to
How fortunate to be free
to write of cars and wars, truths and eras,
throw away old useless
ties and pants that don't fit.

Allen Ginsberg, *White Shroud: Poems 1980–1985*

JM

Out of the Depths – Prayers for Various Occasions

Out of the depths

The writer Primo Levi records that when he was taken to a concentration camp he was an atheist, and when he survived and emerged to normal life again, he was still an atheist. He wrote that he was once tempted to pray – when he knew that at the next moment he would be selected for death or for life. But he felt that to pray at such a moment would be dishonest – and to whom could he pray and how could he live with himself afterwards if he had "cheated" in such a way. Most of us are not so consistent or "pious" as this "unbeliever". Prayer in a time of trouble, even if we have never done so before, is a natural human reaction and one of which we need not be embarrassed. Whether it grows out of a regular prayer life and a sense of communion with God, or is a spontaneous cry out of the night of suffering, it is an urge and experience as old as human society.

One of the greatest records of human prayer is the Book of Psalms, and in times of suffering it may provide the words of prayer that we cannot compose ourselves. We offer here a small selection of prayers derived from it, and have added others from later Jewish tradition.

The great Hasidic master, Nachman of Bratzlav, suggested that reading the Psalms should be a regular part of our spiritual life. For he said:

> Every single person, according to what they are, is able to find himself or herself within the book of Psalms, and earn *teshuvah* (turning and returning to God) through reading the Psalms.

(The references to the verse numbers of the Psalms follow the text of the Hebrew Bible and are sometimes slightly different from the numbering in English Bibles.)

How to Get Up When Life Gets You Down

WHEN OUR WORLD FALLS APART:

Save me, O God,
for the waters have come up to my neck.
I am drowning in deep mire
and there is no foothold.
I have come into deep waters
and the flood is sweeping over me.
I am weary with crying,
my throat is parched.
My eyes grow dim
waiting for God.

PSALM 69:1–3

WHEN BURDENED WITH PERSONAL TROUBLES:

Take pity on me God, take pity,
for in You my soul has taken refuge.
I take refuge in the shadow of Your wings
until the storms are past.

PSALM 57:1

AT A TIME OF A NATURAL DISASTER:

God is our refuge and strength,
an ever-present help in trouble.
Therefore we shall not fear though the earth is changed
and the mountains fall into the depths of the sea;
even though its waters roar and foam
though the mountains shake as they swell.

There is a river whose waters give joy to the city of God,
the holy place of the presence of God.
God is within, it cannot be shaken.
God will help it at the dawning of the day.

PSALM 46:2–6

Out of the depths

IN TIMES OF PERSECUTION:

Be gracious to me, O God,
for men trample upon me;
all day long foes attack me.
My enemies trample upon me all day long
so many attacking me.

When I am afraid
I put my trust in You;
in God whose word I praise.
In God I trust, no longer afraid.
What can mere flesh and blood do to me!

PSALM 56:2–5

FOR LETTING OFF STEAM!

O God, smash their teeth in their mouths,
tear out the fangs of the young lions!
Let them vanish like water that runs away;
when they arm their bows, let them cut themselves to
    pieces!
Let them be like a snail, dissolving into slime,
like a stillborn mole, never seeing the sun!

PSALM 58:7–9

AT MOMENTS OF FEAR:

I lift up my eyes to the hills
where shall I find my help?
My help is from God alone,
maker of heaven and earth.
God will not allow your foot to slip,
for your guardian does not slumber.
Know that the guardian of Israel
never slumbers and never sleeps.
God is your guardian
God is your shade at your right hand.

How to Get Up When Life Gets You Down

The sun will not strike you by day
nor the moon by night.
God will guard you from all harm,
guarding your soul.
God will guard your going out and your coming in
now and for evermore.

PSALM 121

IN EXILE:

As a deer longs for running streams,
so my soul longs for You, my God.
My soul thirsts for God, the living God,
"When shall I come and appear before God?"
My tears have been my food, by day and night,
as all day long they say to me, "Where is your God?"
Why are you cast down my soul,
and why do you moan within me?
Hope in God!
I praise You still,
my own salvation, and my God.

PSALM 42:2–4,12

IN DISTRESS AND FEELING FORSAKEN:

God, in You I have taken refuge,
let me never be ashamed.
Do not cast me off in old age,
when my strength is feeble, do not abandon me.

PSALM 71:1,9

AFTER THE LOSS OF ONE WE LOVE:

Be kind to me, O God, for I am weak,
heal me, for I am torn apart,
my soul is deeply torn,
O God, how long?

184

Out of the depths

Turn to me, God, and save my life,
rescue me through Your faithful love,
for in death there is no memory of You,
in the grave who can praise You.
I am worn out with my moaning,
I flood my bed each night with tears,
I drench my couch with my weeping.
My eye wastes away because of grief,
growing weak because of my troubles.

God has heard my supplication,
God accepts my prayer.

PSALM 6:3–8,10

IN DESPAIR:

Do not forsake me, O God,
O God, be not far from me!
Make haste to help me,
God of my safety.

PSALM 38:22–23

IN NEED OF COMFORT:

The Lord is my shepherd
I shall not want.
In green fields God lets me lie
leading me by quiet streams
restoring my soul,
guiding me in paths of truth,
for such is God's name.

Though I walk through the valley of the shadow of death
I fear no harm
for You are beside me;
Your rod and staff
they comfort me.
You spread a table before me
in front of my enemies.

You soothe my head with oil;
my cup runs over.
Surely goodness and mercy seek me
all the days of my life
and I shall dwell in the house of God forever.

PSALM 23

STRUGGLING WITH THE EVIL WITHIN US:

Sin speaks to the evil,
deep in my heart;
there is no dread of God
within its eyes.

It flatters him too much in his own eyes
to detect and hate his guilt.
The words of his mouth become mischief and deceit,
the urge for wisdom and goodness is gone.
He thinks up mischief as he lies in bed.
He is set on a way that is not good.
He does not reject evil.

God, Your love reaches to heaven,
Your faithfulness to the skies,
Your righteousness is like the mighty mountains,
Your judgments like the great deep.
God, You save man and beast!
How precious is Your love!
All people can take refuge
in the shelter of Your wings.

Continue Your love to those who love You,
and Your faithfulness to the upright in heart.
Let not the foot of pride crush me,
nor the hand of wickedness drive me away.
The wicked deeds have fallen, there they lie,
flung down, they cannot rise again.

PSALM 36:2–8,11–13

Out of the depths

Be kind to me, God, in Your mercy,
in Your great compassion blot out my misdeeds.
Wash me free from my guilt
and cleanse me from my sin
For my misdeeds I know too well
and my sin is always before me.
Against You, You only, have I sinned,
and done what is evil in Your sight.
Therefore You are just in Your sentence,
and right in Your judgment . . .

Purify me with hyssop, and I shall be clean,
wash me, and I shall be whiter than snow.
Let me hear joy and gladness,
so that the bones You crushed dance again.
Turn Your gaze away from my sins
and blot out all my guilt.
Create a pure heart for me, God,
and put a firm and steadfast spirit in me.
Do not cast me away from Your presence,
nor take Your holy spirit from me . . .

For You desire no sacrifice, or I would give it,
burnt offerings You do not want.
God's sacrifices are a humbled spirit,
a broken and contrite heart You will not despise.

PSALM 51:3–6,9–13,18–19

ADMITTING WE'VE DONE WRONG:

When I did not admit it, my body wasted away,
through my groaning all day long.
For day and night Your hand was heavy upon me,
my freshness was replaced
by the dryness of summer.

But when I admit my fault,
and do not hide my guilt,
when I say, I will confess my wrongdoing to God,
then You take away my guilt and my fault.

PSALM 32:3–5

WHEN LIFE LOSES ITS MEANING:

God, let me know my end,
and what is the measure of my days;
how short-lived I am.
See, You have made my days a few hand-breadths,
and my lifetime is as nothing before You.
Surely everyone who stands is a mere breath!
People go around like a shadow,
full of turmoil for nothing,
busily heaping things up,
not knowing who will gather them . . .

Hear my prayer, O God,
give ear to my cry,
do not be silent at my tears.
For I am a stranger with You,
a passing guest like all those before me.
Release me, that I may regain my strength,
before I depart and am no more.

PSALM 39:5–7,13–14

SEEKING GOD:

God, you are my God,
with longing do I seek You.
My soul is thirsty for You,
my flesh is pining for You
in a dry and weary land
where there is no water.

So I looked for You in the holy place,
to see Your power and glory.
Because Your love is better than life,
my lips shall praise You.
So I bless You as long as I live,
in Your name I raise my hands in prayer.

PSALM 63:1–4

WAITING FOR GOD:

Out of the depths I called to You, O God,
God hear my voice.
Let Your ears listen
to the voice of my pleading.

God, if You should mark faults,
O God, who could stand?
But with You there is forgiveness,
for this You are held in awe.

I hope in God,
my soul has hope,
and for God's word I wait.
My soul waits for God
more than watchmen for the morning,
watching for the morning.

PSALM 130:1–6

Jewish tradition is rich in the prayers of individuals and communities. Some are very specialized, depending on a whole structure of belief to make sense, but others speak out very directly to anyone who wishes to use them. Many of the following ones come from the fixed liturgy, though at all times Jews have created their own spontaneous prayers as they stood before God. The power of that personal plea to God is expressed in the following words that come from the Hasidic tradition, the Pietist movement of the eighteenth century in Eastern Europe.

Let each of us cry out and lift our heart to God, as if we were hanging by a hair, and a tempest were raging to the very heart of heaven, and we were at a loss for what to do, and there were hardly time to cry out. It is a time when no counsel, indeed, can help us and we have no refuge save to remain in our loneliness, and lift our eyes and our heart up and cry out to God. And this should be done at all times, for in the world we are in great danger.

To this advice we should add the words of Nachman of Bratzlav:

This whole world is nothing but a very narrow bridge – but the essential thing is never to be afraid.

A MORNING PRAYER

My God, the soul You have given me is pure, for You created it, You formed it and You made it live within me. You watch over it within me, but one day You will take it from me to everlasting life. My God and God of my ancestors, as long as the soul is within me, I will declare that You are the power of good deeds, the ruler of all creatures, possessing every soul. Blessed are You, who brings the dead into everlasting life.

Traditional Prayer

A PRAYER FOR COURAGE

Our God and God of our ancestors, help us to live according to Your teaching and to hold fast to Your commands. Let us not come into the power of sin or wrongdoing, temptation or disgrace. Let no evil within us control us, and keep us far from bad people and bad company. Help us hold fast to the good within us and to good deeds, and bend our will and our desires to serve You. Give us today and every day, grace, kindness and mercy in Your sight and in the sight of all who regard us, and grant us Your love and kindness.

Traditional Prayer

Out of the depths

AN EVENING PRAYER

Source of our life and our Sovereign, cause us to lie down in peace and rise again to enjoy life. Spread over us the covering of Your peace, guide us with Your good counsel and save us for the sake of Your name. Be a shield about us, turning away every enemy, disease, violence, hunger and sorrow. Shelter us in the shadow of Your wings, for You are a God who guards and protects us, a ruler of mercy and compassion. Guard us when we go out and when we come in, to enjoy life and peace both now and forevermore, and spread over us the shelter of Your peace.

Traditional Prayer

A PRAYER OF HOPE

This prayer was found written on the walls of a cellar in Cologne, Germany, where Jews had been hiding from the Nazis.

> I believe in the sun though it doesn't shine.
> I believe in love even though I don't feel it.
> I believe in God though he is silent.

SEEKING AND FINDING GOD

> God, where shall I find You?
> High and hidden is Your place.
> And where shall I not find You?
> The world is full of Your glory.
>
> I have sought Your nearness,
> With all my heart I called You
> and going out to meet You
> I found You coming to meet me.

Judah Halevi (12th-century Spain)

ON SUFFERING

I do not beg You to reveal to me the secret of Your ways – I could not bear it. But show me one thing; show it to me more clearly and more deeply: show me what this, which is happening at this very moment, means to me, what it demands of me, what You, Lord of the world, are telling me by way of it. Ah, it is not why I suffer, that I wish to know, but only whether I suffer for Your sake.

Levi Yitzhak of Berditchev (18th-century Hasidic master)

PRAYING FOR INTEGRITY

Give us integrity to love You and fear You. So shall we never lose our self-respect, nor be put to shame, for You are the power which works to save us.

Traditional Prayer

May the words of my mouth and the thoughts within my heart, be acceptable to You, O God, my rock and my redeemer.

PSALM 19:15

BEFORE AN OPERATION

Before my operation I turn to You, because You are always beside me.

You created the healing powers of my body and the strength and courage of my spirit. They are Your gifts to carry me from fear to confidence.

Yours are the wonder of science and the marvel of creation. I thank You for the wisdom of my doctors, the skill of my surgeon's hands and the devotion of my nurses. They are Your helpers in the work of healing. They comfort me.

God, I am Your child whom You created. God lead me gently into sleep and waken me to health. In Your love I trust.

Reform Synagogues Prayer Book

Out of the depths

As a child turns to his father or mother, I turn to You, my God who created me. You are the master of my life and my death, may it be Your will to heal me and keep me in life. But if it is time for me to go forward through death to life everlasting, give me courage and trust to ease my journey.

Forgive my sins, and my soul will be pure as it returns to You. Protect those I love whom I leave behind, for their lives are in Your care. Through Your mercy we shall come together in the gathering of life. In Your hand I lay my soul, when I sleep and when I wake, and with my soul my body too. You are with me, I shall not fear.

Reform Synagogues Prayer Book

PRAYING FOR OTHERS

For those who are ill
God, I pray for . . . who is sick and in pain. May it be Your will to renew his/her strength and bring him/her back to health. Renew his/her spirit also and free him/her from anxiety for You watch over his/her body and his/her soul.

Though I cannot share his/her pain, help me to bring him/her good cheer and comfort. Give us the joy of helping each other through all the fortunes of life.

Blessed are You, God, the faithful and merciful healer.

Reform Synagogues Prayer Book

ON BEHALF OF THE DANGEROUSLY ILL

I pray to You for . . . who approaches the frontiers of this life. You are the master over life and death and his/her fate is in Your hands. Heal his/her body and restore him/her to me, if this is Your will. If it is not, be with him/her where I cannot follow, and give him/her courage to conquer pain, and hope to overcome fear. Lead him/her forwards in peace from this world into the life that has no end, supported by his/her own good deeds, and accompanied by my love. Help me too, and teach me that though we may part now, we shall come together once again in the gathering of life. His/Her soul is in Your hand, and with his/her soul, his/her body too. You are with him/her, I shall not fear.

Reform Synagogues Prayer Book

JM

A Non-Pious Postscript

A non-pious postscript

In the book of Deuteronomy we are told that if we are good, and do God's will, He will send us in return rain for our crops and pasture for our cattle, i.e. prosperity. The good life will lead to good living.

But life doesn't work like that, and the great theme in the rest of the Bible concerns why it doesn't and what we should do about it. Why do the wicked prosper? Why does Job suffer? Who is the suffering servant of Isaiah? Is suffering a secret blessing? Will another world redress the injustices of this one? Only bits of answers are provided but it is through battling with these problems that religion deepens and people become profound. The cosmos ceases to be a simple morality fable. It now includes tragedy, comedy, darkness, and light beyond our imagining, all interwoven curiously and perplexingly. The cosmos is working something out within us as well as outside us. With our consent or without it, we are the stage on which it happens. We are also the actors and the audience. Perhaps we also contribute to the script and influence the ending.

"Into each life, some rain must fall", says a popular song. For some of us, that rain is a storm so violent it extinguishes our life, for some it is just an irritating sprinkle. There is no life without it. It seems random, erratic, wasteful, purposeless, teasing and sadistic, and many theologians expend enormous amounts of concentration trying to tidy up the mess and the squalid magnificence it leaves behind.

In this book, Jonathan and I have not tried to tidy up that mess. We have not packaged suffering up in shiny paper, and tied it up with a pious bow. Alzheimers, AIDS and concentration camps are not presented as divinity in disguise but as the dreadful nightmares that people have had to wake up to.

The purpose of this book is to show that whatever your suffering, other people have been there before you, and to give examples of what, if anything, they made out of it and with it. And also where their ingenuity and wisdom came to a full stop, if and how they could accept such blackness, waste and pain.

Actually they made such a lot out of it and with it, that this book is a testimony to the power of the spirit, whether we label it human, divine or both, its creativity and its resilience. It is also a testimony to the tragedies we inflict on ourselves and on each other. Humour is not produced by happiness, but in battle with its opposite. So it is with courage, spirituality, and true love. The choice between creation and destruction is always there and they are the fruits of the tension.

An example! I am part of a religious establishment, a religious bureaucrat for over forty years. I have become over-familiar with liturgy, having written such a lot of it and I can no longer feel it. I no longer want to herd the faithful into prayer meetings, or monitor the "progress" of institutions, I need renewal myself.

In the last few years, my renewal has come from retreats which I have "conducted" for the terminally ill, alcoholics, HIV carriers, and AIDS sufferers. I have put "conducted" in inverted commas, because the retreatants conducted me back to belief, and goodness. Their devastating honesty gave me courage to be angry and use four-letter words about Whomever and Whatever organizes the cosmos (it could have been organized better). They led me back to spirituality and love of life beyond the body and to what grows out of disintegration. The sources of my religion and strength are marginalized, suffering people.

Now why this should be so is a great mystery, it is perhaps the point of the play that is performed with us and in us, as I've said. Those caught up in it have insights, and answers (though not The Answer). You who read this book must have them both within you too, for you must also suffer, no one is exempt from it. You can check your own insights and answers against those in this book.

If they deepen them and extend them, and make them more practical and illuminate them with unexpected shafts of light, and disconcerting cackles of laughter, if they make you more interested in and more objective about your own suffering, then this book has served its purpose.

My grandfather used to sigh in Yiddish, "It's hard to be a Jew!" I think it's hard to be a human being, but like him, I'm not going to opt out – it's awful and fascinating but at least you don't die of boredom.

Lionel Blue